# FIRST *and* SECOND KINGS

# FIRST *and* SECOND KINGS

*By*

RICHARD I. McNEELY

**MOODY PRESS**

**CHICAGO**

**Library of Congress Cataloging in Publication Data**

McNeely, Richard I., 1928-
  First and Second Kings.
  Bibliography: p. 157.
  1. Bible. O.T. Kings—Commentaries.

BS1335.3.M32          222'.5'07          77-29039

ISBN 0-8024-2011-7

# Contents

# Foreword

It is generally known among students of the Bible that there is a serious lack of bibliography on the books of Kings. This stems from two reasons: (1) the popular concept that history is uninteresting, and (2) the failure to realize that spiritual principles and values pervade all history. History is God's operation in human life and reveals His effective accomplishment of His program for His glory.

Dr. Richard I. McNeely is well qualified to treat these books. As Chairman and Professor of Bible at Biola College, he is the popular instructor of large classes of college students in a department that is one of the largest in the college. His academic and theological preparation for the task is superb. In addition, he has served with distinction in the United States Navy as a chaplain (he maintains reserve status), and has to his credit a number of years of college teaching. He is much sought after for his public ministry to youth and adults.

This work correctly reveals the significance of the books of Kings. 1) It demonstrates that the contents are the backbone for the history of the monarchy in Israel and Judah. 2) It clearly shows that the history is the matrix of the messages of the prophets (comparable to the relation of the book of Acts to the Pauline epistles). 3) Its underscores God's preparation of His people for Messiah's presentation of Himself as King. 4) It carefully emphasizes and illustrates many spiritual principles contained in the Mosaic Law and throughout the Scriptures. 5) It stresses the sovereignty of God, who sets up and puts down rulers of earth. 6) It has polemic and apologetic value in the defense of the sacred record by the help of archaeology and a valid chronology. 7) It rightly includes certain historical material gleaned from contemporary events among Israel's neighbors.

The purpose of the volume is to provide a pedagogically helpful text for colleges and other schools in a field where students come with little or no preparation.

The student will find good outlines to guide him to the mastery of the contents of the books. A selective and suggestive (not exhaustive) bibliography is included to help students in further study. In view of the paucity of recent works on the important books of Kings, this volume is welcome and will make a valuable contribution to the literature on these vital books of Scripture.

CHARLES LEE FEINBERG

# Introduction

"Now King David was old, advanced in age" (1 Kings 1:1). With these words the history of the decline and fall of Israel begins. The books of 1 and 2 Kings synthesize the history of the territorial expansion of Israel under the rule of David's son, Solomon, and then trace the dissolution of that kingdom at Solomon's death. The strength of the Davidic throne needed more than territorial or military greatness. Its power lay in the spiritual resources promised to Israel by the covenant-keeping God, Jehovah. These resources were squandered by Solomon through his alliances with pagan nations, and this wasting of spiritual resources carried on into the time recorded in these two books.

## THE SIGNIFICANCE OF THE BOOKS OF KINGS

The apostle Paul, commenting on the experiences of the children of Israel and their record of spiritual decline during the wilderness wanderings, observes, "Now these things happened to them as an example, and they were written for our instruction, upon whom the ends of the ages have come" (1 Cor 10:11). If this is true of the events described in the Pentateuch, then it follows that the history recorded in Kings is also significant. These books present God as sovereign over all man's affairs, God as faithful to His people, and man as responsible for his actions.

### THE SOVEREIGN GOD

God was in charge. The role of the prophet in announcing God's directive predominates. What God purposes to happen, happens. This was demonstrated by a number of events. By the prophet Ahijah the Lord announced to Jeroboam the coming

division (1 Kings 11:29-32). By another prophet He foretold
the penalty that would be exacted for Jeroboam's erecting the
false altar. He prophesied the birth of a Judahite king, Josiah,
who would be God's retributive instrument in the future (1 Kings
13:1-4). Mention could be made of Micaiah's prophecy concerning battle against the Syrians (1 Kings 22:13-28), Elijah's word
to Ahaziah of his impending death, and Elisha's encounters with
the king of Syria (2 Kings 6:8-19). All of these are reminders
that the God of Israel "slumbers not nor sleeps."

THE FAITHFUL GOD

The books of Kings call attention to a second attribute of
God—His faithfulness. Sometimes stated (1 Kings 11:31-36),
often implied, God was faithful in spite of the apostate actions of
His people. He offered them many opportunities for spiritual renewal. Even in Israel, which was never led by a godly king in its
two hundred years of existence, there were seven thousand who
did not bow the knee to Baal (1 Kings 19:18). Judah experienced at least five periods of reformation led by kings who in
many cases had long reigns, thus assuring some continuity to the
reform movements.

MAN AS A RESPONSIBLE BEING

All through Kings, man is depicted as responsible for his ob-
stinancy and rebellion. Man is always aware that the decisions
he makes in life are his decisions. That is the human side to
which Paul alludes in Romans 10, and he indicts Israel for her
unbelief. Israel was culpable before God for her own behavior.
One has only to read the section that explains the causes for captivity to see the responsibility placed upon man.

But how does one reconcile God's sovereignty and man's responsibility? Charles Spurgeon was once asked that question,
and his response was, "One has no need to reconcile friends."
Certainly both are taught in the Scriptures, and somewhere there

is a reconciliation in the mind of God. No doubt the apostle Paul was referring to that seeming problem as he wrote: "Oh, the depth of the riches both of the wisdom and knowledge of God! How unsearchable are His judgments and unfathomable His ways!" (Rom 11:33).

## THE AUTHORSHIP

The human authorship of 1 and 2 Kings is not known. Obviously, whoever did the final work on Kings had a great number of resources available to him. Several ideas concerning authorship have evolved. Almost all commentators agree that much of the material contained in the books was compiled prior to the exile, but that the copy in final form was the work of someone or ones during the exile. Most attach importance to the relationship between Kings and the covenant agreements specified in Deuteronomy. At this point, however, there is some disagreement. John Gray, who also cites a number of others, believes the book was the work of a priest. In a footnote he explains:

> Priestly authorship is suggested by the fact that the characteristic feature is criticism of the cult in the monarchy and that generally the only persons named besides kings and queen-mothers are priests.[1]

It could be that a priest was responsible for the final redaction, but Gray overlooks the emphasis also given prophets in the work. The appearance of Nathan is followed by the notation of prophetic sources such as Gad (1 Chron 29:29), Ahijah and Iddo (2 Chron 9:29), Jehu (1 Kings 16:1-4), not to mention Micaiah (1 Kings 22) and the great sagas of Elijah and Elisha (1 Kings 17 ff.). Certainly, the prophets had as much interest in the affairs of state as the priests. Edwin R. Thiele presents the most plausible argument for the work being largely prophetic and based on the Deuteronomic tradition.[2] This is far more likely when recording

---

1. John Gray, *I and II Kings*, p. 6.
2. Edwin R. Thiele, *The Mysterious Numbers of the Hebrew Kings*, p. 177.

events in the Northern Kingdom since there was hardly a functioning priesthood there.

Whom could one suggest as the final redactor? It could have been Ezra, a priest, who had a strong feeling for the history of the people. Just as likely it could have been either the prophet Ezekiel or the prophet Jeremiah.*[3]

## THE PLAN OF THE BOOKS

First Kings opens with a reference to the last days of David the king and to the rivalries sparked by his imminent demise (1 Kings 1-2). After recording the establishment of Solomon, the author details the events and characteristics that marked Solomon's reign (1 Kings 3-11). Having noted the reasons for the dissolution of the united kingdom, the author then traces the history of the kings of both the Northern and Southern divisions. The division of the kingdom into two weaker units was an important factor in the fortunes of each as they sometimes stood against each other and at other times were bound together in a common cause.

Second Kings begins with what might appear to be an interruption in the flow of the book. At this point the final days of Elijah and the commencement of Elisha's ministry are recorded. Elisha's death is noted in 2 Kings 13:20. Brief accounts of subsequent kings of Israel and Judah follow.

The books were not written merely to recount the history of the people of Israel. To read them through (especially at a single sitting) is to discover what James A. Montgomery has described:

> The Book is a history written with a religious theory and a political aim. It has for subject not mere History, but the lessons of History. There is honest self-judgment in this period of Hebrew historiography. The schism of Israel from the God-ordained Davidic kingdom was due to Solomon's sins, the fall

---

*If one follows the argument of Wallace Stearns, either one of these would be strong candidates.

3. *International Standard Bible Encyclopedia*, s.v. "Books of Kings."

of the North to its continued defiance of the True Religion, and again the ruin of Judah to the inescapable fate deserved by Manasseh's sin. The remarkable note is that, when all was lost, some one found the history of that tragic period worth recording as a lesson of God's discipline of his people.[4]

## THE COMPARISON WITH THE CHRONICLES

One who is familiar with both Kings and Chronicles, may question God's purpose for including both books in the canon. Certainly the books are similar, but not identical. We may learn something from the place the Jews gave to each of these books in the Hebrew Scriptures. The books of Kings belonged to the portion of Scripture termed the "prophets." Chronicles was placed with Psalms, Proverbs, and other books referred to as the "writings."

Chronicles views the span of history covered by the Kings from a southern, or Judean bias. The writer, whom ancient Jewish tradition alleges to have been Ezra, considers the Northern Kingdom important only in its contact with Judah. His taking this view was occasioned by Israel's disregard of God's authority, evidenced by idolatrous worship and disregard of the prophets sent to her. Simply, Chronicles reveals the history of the people of Israel from the priestly or Temple viewpoint.

The book of Chronicles begins with the reign of David, although it does trace the genealogy of the twelve tribes over which David ruled. Clearly, the work was written to develop the history of the Davidic dynasty, and to give an account of each ruler in comparison with the dynasty's progenitor.

Each king was also evaluated not on the basis of his personal characteristics, but on the basis of his attitude toward the Temple. David's great zeal to build a permanent house for the worship of Jehovah was the basis for Solomon's actual construction of it.

4. James A. Montgomery, *A Critical and Exegetical Commentary on the Books of Kings*, pp. 44-45.

But Solomon was not the touchstone for one's evaluation of the Temple; David was. David's preparation for Temple building was emphasized (1 Chron 22:1-5). David commissioned his son Solomon to build the center (1 Chron 22:6-16). David announced to the people that Solomon would construct the Temple (1 Chron 28), and Solomon attributed the plan to erect it to David (2 Chron 6:4-8). Every succeeding king of Judah, therefore, was considered in light of his devotion to the worship of Jehovah. A monarch's inner worship would be evidenced by his concern for the priesthood and the Temple in which it functioned. For example, Rehoboam "did evil because he did not set his heart to seek the LORD" (2 Chron 12:14). Hezekiah "did what was good, right, and true before the LORD his God. And every work which he began in the service of the house of God in law and in commandment, seeking his God, he did with all his heart and prospered" (2 Chron 31:20-21).

## PROBLEMS IN CHRONOLOGY

No more perplexing problem faces the student of the book of Kings than the chronology of the rulers. What appears to be simple as one reads the text does not balance when the numbers are counted. The problem lies principally in the addition of the years of Judah's kings. Most historians agree that these kings must be placed within a time range of 931 B.C. to 605 B.C., or a period of approximately 325 years. But the years of the Judean kings total about 388.

Three solutions have been suggested. One is the possibility of *coregencies*. (A coregency is a shared rule. A nation under a coregency is usually governed by two rulers, often a father and son.) For example, there is little doubt that Uzziah was crowned king in 790 B.C. after his father Amaziah had reigned only six years. But the Scripture notes that Amaziah's reign covered a period of fifty-two years (2 Kings 15:1-2). Regarding this period of Judah's history, Gleason L. Archer demonstrates that in the years between 743 B.C. and 739 B.C., "Judah was ruled over by no less than three kings at once: Uzziah, Jotham, and Ahaz."[5]

A second explanation is that *calendar reckoning* differed. Thiele asks the fundamental question: When did a king begin counting the years of his reign? He then demonstrates how Israel and Judah employed two different means of determining regal years:

> The methods employed by Israel and Judah in the reckoning of the reigns of their kings would thus be as follows: Israel at the time of the schism followed the nonaccession-year system and continued its use till the close of the ninth century B.C. when under Jehoash a shift was made to the accession-year system, which continued to be used to the close of Israel's history. Judah at the time of the schism used the accession-year system and continued its use to the middle of the ninth century; from Jehoram to Joash reigns are reckoned according to the non-accession-year system; and from Amaziah, at about the beginning of the eighth century, to the close of Judah's history the accession-year system was again in use.[6]

This means that when computing the number of years a king reigned, the *accession year* was counted as a whole year even if he had ascended the throne on the last day of the calendar year. In the nonaccession-year system, the dating of the reign began with the first full year's reign.

A third explanation offered as a solution to the chronology problem is that *calendar year beginnings* differed in the Northern and Southern Kingdoms. The Northern Kingdom began its calendar year in the spring with the first month of the religious year—the month of Nisan, or Abib. Judah began its calendar year with the seventh month of the religious year—the period normally considered as New Year (Rosh Hashana) by Jewish people today.

5. Gleason L. Archer, *A Survey of Old Testament Introduction*, p. 279.
6. Thiele, p. 38.

The problems of chronology are further answered by other sources dealing with this time period.[7]

## THE SIGNIFICANT DATES

Several significant dates must be remembered in order to better understand 1 and 2 Kings. We should realize that all dates are subject to review, and that authors differ in their views. The following general outline, suggested by Montgomery, is in general agreement with major dates in Thiele,[8] Archer,[9] and Samuel J. Schultz.[10]

931 B.C.-Division of the Kingdom
722 B.C.-Fall of the Northern Kingdom, Assyrian Captivity
605 B.C.-Judah subjugated by Nebuchadnezzar
587 B.C.-Jerusalem destroyed, Babylonian Captivity[11]

Others, following Albright, have arrived at some variant dates.[12] The differences in dating are relatively minor in importance. Only the date of the division of the kingdom is seriously questioned. Some assign it as 922 B.C. rather than 931 B.C.

## THE PROPHETS OF ISRAEL

The history of David's rule indicates that the prophet Nathan ranked among David's most wise and trusted counselors. God had seemingly guaranteed a spokesman for Israel when He promised Moses that He would raise up a replacement. This prophecy marks a line of prophets that culminated in Jesus Christ.

This period in Israel's history did not lack words from God. Over twenty prophets spoke or wrote during the period although

7. David Alexander and Pat Alexander, eds., *Eerdmans' Handbook to the Bible*, pp. 270-71.
8. Thiele, p. 53 ff.
9. Archer, p. 280.
10. Samuel J. Schultz, *The Old Testament Speaks*, p. 154.
11. Montgomery, pp. 58-64.
12. J. A. Thompson, *The Bible and Archaeology*, p. 118.

not all are mentioned in 1 and 2 Kings. Nathan continued his ministry to the Davidic dynasty and showed his loyalty to David by insuring the coronation of Solomon as David's rightful heir to the throne. As Solomon's reign came to its closing days, Ahijah delivered to Jeroboam God's message concerning the rebellion that was arising and from which Jeroboam would gain a kingdom.

Much of the content of the latter part of 1 Kings, as well as the opening chapters of 2 Kings, relates to the exploits of Elijah and Elisha. And who could not be moved by the tenacity for God that marked the prophetic declarations of Micaiah (1 Kings 22:8-28)? The effect of Isaiah is realized when 2 Kings 18:13—20:19 is compared with Isaiah 36:1—39:8. Assuming the date suggested above for the writing of 1 and 2 Kings, it is not difficult to believe that the writer utilized verbatim the material Isaiah had incorporated into his prophecy.

In some instances the prophet was not identified, for the spokesman was not as important as the word from God (cf. 2 Kings 21:10-11).

# FIRST AND SECOND KINGS
## An Overview

| B.C. 971 | B.C. 971-931 | B.C. 931-874 | B.C. 874-853 |
|---|---|---|---|
| THE LAST DAYS OF DAVID THE KING | SOLOMON IN ALL HIS GLORY | DIVISION, HOSTILITY, AND CONSOLIDATION | ELIJAH AND THE REIGN OF AHAB |
| *Chapter One* | *Chapter Two* | *Chapter Three* | *Chapter Four* |
| 1 Kings 1:1— 2:12 | 1 Kings 2:13— 11:43 | 1 Kings 12:1— 16:28 | 1 Kings 16:29— 22:40 |
| The Shunammite Rebellion of Adonijah Coronation of Solomon David's Instructions to Solomon David's Death | Establishment of Power Endowment of Wisdom Organization of the Kingdom Building of the Temple Solomon's Residence The Temple Furnishings The Dedication of the Temple Solomon's Wealth, Glory, and Honor Solomon's Apostasy and Decline | Disruption of the Kingdom at Shechem Beginnings of the Israelite Kingdom The Southern Loyalists Revolution in Israel | Beginning Ministry of the Prophet Elijah The Israelite-Syrian Wars |

# FIRST AND SECOND KINGS
## An Overview

| B.C. 853-841 | B.C. 841-722 | B.C. 796-568 |
|---|---|---|
| Elisha, the Man of the Spirit | Israel's Decline and Disaster | Recovery, Reform, Relapse, and Ruin |
| *Chapter Five* | *Chapter Six* | *Chapter Seven* |
| 1 Kings 22:40— 2 Kings 9:13 | 2 Kings 9:1— 17:41 | 2 Kings 14:1— 25:30 |
| Historical Setting Elisha's Ministry to Israel | Dynasty of Jehu The Final Kings God's Vindication of His Judgment The Development of Samaritan Religion | The Reign of Amaziah The Reign of Azariah The Reign of Jotham The Reign of Ahaz The Reign of Hezekiah The Beginning of the End The Eye of the Storm The Renewed Fury and Destruction |

# 1

## The Last Days of David the King

### 1 Kings 1:1—2:12

In the first ten chapters of 2 Samuel, David's career seems to have been a continuum of victory, kindness, and enlargement. Then on impulse, David summoned the beautiful Bathsheba to his palace, committed adultery, and tried to cover the deed by murdering Uriah, her husband.

The Davidic fortunes began their downward plunge. Amnon raped his half-sister; Absalom avenged her shame by murdering Amnon. Absalom went into exile. When he returned to the court, he plotted against his father. David, forced into exile, suffered indignities from his subjects. Distresesd by Joab's murder of Absalom, David returned to his capital. Second Samuel closes with David having caused a plague that killed seventy thousand Israelites. This tragedy was assuaged only by his repentance and sacrificial offerings at the newly purchased threshing floor of Araunah, later to become the site of Israel's center of worship.

The historian is not finished with the tale of David's losses. First Kings opens with a powerless regent, one whose loss of strength and energy all but forced his retirement from public life. History records the accounts of many who, holding titles of great power, nevertheless were forced by physical conditions to surrender their ruling power to advisors around them. This was true of David.

The section from 1:1 to 2:12 presents a synopsis of the events that ended David's reign and secured the throne for Solomon. The account begins with the rather strange situation of the service of a Shunammite, moves through Adonijah's attempted coup d' état and his request to marry the Shunammite, his death, and the Solomonic party's victory over the rivals.

## THE SHUNAMMITE

### 1 Kings 1:2-12

Abishag, the Shunammite, was acclaimed as the most beautiful girl in the land. Her presence in the court was the result of a national search that finally brought the king's servants to her village, Shunem, located some seven miles southeast of Nazareth in the northern section of the country. The town later became famous for it was here that Elisha brought a woman's son to life (2 Kings 4:12-37).

The appearance of Abishag is important to the rapid rise and fall of Adonijah whose career is recounted next. Her service to David was to supply warmth to his body, a therapeutic remedy attested by the Jewish historian Josephus and the Greek physician Galen.[1] In David's case, the treatment was suggested by his counselors who no doubt feared open power struggles brought on by the loss of David's virility.

Her service to the king was one of nursing, and the historian quickly noted it was only that. This is not to be taken as a note of David's purity, but rather of the extent of his weakness. The tendency is to read this passage in light of Western culture. David had already taken several wives and concubines into his harem, and seemingly Abishag was added to that number.

---

1. James A. Montgomery, *A Critical and Exegetical Commentary on the Books of Kings,* pp. 71-72.

## THE REBELLION OF ADONIJAH

### 1 Kings 1:5-31

THE CONSPIRATORS

Adonijah was the fourth and probably the oldest surviving son of David (2 Sam 3:4). With such status, he felt that he was the rightful heir to his father's throne. He was supported in his claim by two of David's most trusted deputies, Joab and Abiathar. Joab, David's nephew (1 Chron 2:16), served as David's military commander. But Joab also had been in the front lines of former court intrigue. His mediation had prepared the way for Absalom to reenter court life—a move that opened the way for Absalom's coup. Then, against the king's orders, Joab had slain Absalom (2 Sam 18:5-15).

Abiathar had been a companion and close confidant of David before he was elevated to the throne. Abiathar had escaped Saul's purge of the priests at Nob and, because of his loyalty, was well received in the royal palace. He rendered service as a counselor.

In preparation for his succession to the throne, Adonijah readied a retinue of fifty chariots and horsemen. Gray has suggested that these were employed "ostensibly to enhance his [Adonijah's] prestige, but probably in anticipation of a coup d' état."[2] Participation in a common meal had the effect of uniting his followers in the cause to which they were dedicated. The tragic note of verse 6 could instruct parents in the necessity of dealing with youngsters. *The Living Bible* paraphrase is poignant: "Now his father, King David, had never disciplined him at any time—not so much as by a single scolding!"

The site of the feast, En-Rogel, was located at the juncture of the valleys of Kidron (Jehoshaphat) and Hinnom. En-Rogel was one of the two springs that supplied water to the Davidic city. En-Rogel was the southern spring, and Gihon was the northern.

2. John Gray, *I and II Kings*, p. 79.

En-Rogel is now known as Job's well, probably indicating a corruption of the name *Joab*.

## THE LOYALISTS

Some leaders in the Davidic court, formidable though few, were not allied with the rebellious party. Verse 8 lists a number of very influential men who were not taken in by the conspiracy. With Nathan the prophet as spokesman, they brought the matter to Bathsheba who in turn provided the hearing before the king. Nathan and Bathsheba were both aware of Solomon's special position. Through Nathan the Lord had named the child Jedidiah, "Beloved of Jehovah" (2 Sam 12:24-25). C. F. Keil accepts this special singling out of David's son as a sign to David that the Lord had chosen Solomon as his successor, even though the oath recorded in verses 13 and 30 had never before appeared.[3]

Nathan's warning was consistent with the tactics of the times. Adonijah's enthronement would have resulted in the deaths of both Bathsheba and Solomon. Gray notes that this was the very purpose of the exclusion of Nathan, Benaiah, and the palace bodyguard, as well as Solomon, from the enthronement feast:

> Adonijah was not prepared for 'peaceful coexistence,' to which, by ancient Semitic convention, he would have been committed by such a meal. He obviously trusted in the strength of his party to liquidate the opposition (cf. v. 12), the strength of which, to say nothing of the weakness of the king, he much underrated.[4]

After Bathsheba had given the king a brief review of the situation, Nathan appeared in court and confirmed the revolutionary activities of Adonijah. Evidently Bathsheba exited the chambers of David at this point. However, she waited nearby to be summoned again and to receive the decision of the frail but function-

3. C. F. Keil and F. Delitzsch, *Biblical Commentary on the Old Testament*, vol. 6, *The Book of Kings*, by C. F. Keil, p. 18.
4. Gray, p. 84.

ing regent. His words declared, "Your son Solomon shall be king after me."

## THE CORONATION OF SOLOMON

After the plot of Adonijah was revealed, David ordered Zadok the priest, Nathan the prophet, and Benaiah the captain of the palace guard to take Solomon to the spring Gihon, located one-half mile (700 meters) north of the festivities hosted by Adonijah. The king gave specific instructions: Solomon was to ride David's mule. This action would indicate not only Solomon's royalty, but also that he was David's own choice of successor. The prophet Nathan was important to the setting as well. To the south, the forces of Adonijah had a military commander and a priest, but no prophet. The place of the prophet was important, and Nathan's presence at the solemn coronation would be evidence of God's favor on the proceedings.

Such a tumult in proximity to the gathering at En-Rogel was bound to attract attention. The spring of En-Rogel was south of the city walls; Gihon was just to the eastern side. To Joab, it sounded as if the whole city were caught up in some kind of excitement. Then Jonathan, the son of the rebellious priest Abiathar, arrived with the news. Recounting the events that occured at Gihon, he added the devastating announcement, "Solomon has even taken his seat on the throne of the kingdom" (v. 46). The enthronement of Solomon was an act of David, and was confirmed by an affirmation of loyalty by the palace servants.

The attempted coup was foiled before it really got started. The principals in the coup reacted in predictable fashion. Panic-stricken, they left the festivities and scattered. Adonijah, sensing that Solomon possibly would deal with him as he had anticipated dealing with Solomon, raced for the altar of burnt offering and laid hold of the "horns of the altar."

On those proturberances from the corners of the altar the sacrificial blood was smeared, representing God's dealing with man's rebellion. Gray states that such a place "afforded sanctuary *par excellence.*"[5] Exodus 21:14 implies that this was a haven of protection until a matter had been investigated and settled. The act was not only a Jewish practice, but was widely accepted among other nations.[6]

Word of Adonijah's action was brought to Solomon and with it a plea that Solomon not avenge the rebellion of Adonijah with death. Solomon assented to this on the condition that Adonijah behave himself and not incur wrath by further rebellious activities. He appeared before the newly enthroned king, and Solomon dismissed him in peace.

### DAVID'S INSTRUCTIONS TO SOLOMON

### 1 Kings 2:1-9

David's instructions to Solomon were twofold. The first related to Solomon's relationship to God (2:2-4), and the second to his dealings with men (2:5-9). These instructions were the last words of a great man. Prior to this, David had delivered his public farewell address (1 Chron 28-29), but the words spoken now were personal. Solomon doubtless regarded his father with reverence; therefore, these words took on special significance. Solomon's humility in viewing his responsibility of rule is well known.

#### SOLOMON'S RELATIONSHIP TO GOD (2:2-4)

Recalling the words of Joshua (Josh 23:14), David beautifully expressed what to him would be a new but soon-to-be-encountered experience: "I am going the way of all the earth." The announcement of his imminent death was followed by two exhortations to Solomon: "Be strong . . . and show yourself a man" and "Keep the charge of the LORD your God." These com-

5. Ibid., p. 96.
6. Ibid.

mands were similar to those the Lord gave Joshua (Josh 1:6-9), as well as to Moses' farewell to Joshua (Deut 31:23).

The first of David's commands to Solomon had *personal integrity* as its core. The Philistines had once encouraged each other with similar words (1 Sam 4:9). Montgomery notes the command is "a veritable soldier's challenge, used by the Philistines in mutual encouragement."[7] Robert Jamieson links it to the apostle Paul's injunction of 1 Corinthians 16:13 in that it "refers to the fortitude or strength of mind that was required to discharge the onerous functions of king."[8]

The second exhortation was more expanded. Personal integrity, presumed to be a prerequisite for keeping God's commands, was not dealt with in a cursory way. Obeying God's commands would keep the kingdom, and David did not wish to overlook this. The command connoted obedience to God in its whole intent and extent. It was expanded to give specificity.

The Hebrew word for "statutes" means "the things engraved." This reflects the means used by God in the production of the Mosaic Law. The *commandments* and *statutes* furnished the direct commands of the Lord to the people of Israel. Jehovah's *ordinances* are referred to by Gray as *"ad hoc* decisions which are accumulated as legal precedents."[9] The last descriptive word, *testimonies,* denotes the imperatives God laid upon His people in light of the first three. Together, the four specifically refer to the legal covenant that bound the people of Israel to God—the covenant delivered through Moses during the traumatic events of the Sinai encampment.

Keeping the commandments of God resulted in great benefits. Solomon was assured of *personal success* if these terms were met. The kind of success that Solomon would enjoy was not automatic.

7. Montgomery, p. 89.
8. Robert Jamieson, "Joshua-Esther," in *A Commentary, Critical, Experimental and Practical on the Old and New Testaments,* by Robert Jamieson, A. R. Fausset, and David Brown, 2:295.
9. Gray, p. 99.

The word used by David indicates that such success was born out of the crucible of difficult experience. Even in the Old Testament, success was recognized to be largely attained on the basis of an intense and active life of devotion, not one of passive perfection. Though the account of Solomon's entire reign is sparse, nevertheless, the accounting of his success is clear.

Second, and of great import, is the word concerning the perpetuity of the Davidic dynasty (2:4). The covenant with the house of David was one of the most important God had made with His people. The Davidic covenant guaranteed three basic promises: an eternal Davidic dynasty, an eternal throne, and an eternal kingdom (2 Sam 7:12 ff.). This covenant agreement was reiterated to Solomon by Jehovah (1 Kings 9:5), and was stated by Gabriel as fulfilled in the birth of Jesus (Luke 1:32-33). Giving the covenant a negative twist, David used it as a stern warning to Solomon that, though the Lord's promise pertained to perpetuity, sin on the part of Davidic posterity would not go unpunished.

SOLOMON'S DEALINGS WITH MEN (2:5-9)

In David's mind, some matters remained to be settled before his death. Therefore three names from the past appear again in the record.

Of these three, Joab was the most recent to the historical setting. Joab's career was spotted. He ascended to the heights of great bravery and descended to the vale of treachery. Through all this, he did give unstinting and loyal service to David. Even when acting in defiance, or at least disregard, of the king's commands, he was never involved in any attempt to overthrow David's power. Unger characterizes him as "one of the most accomplished and unscrupulous warriors that Israel ever produced."[10]

David reminded Solomon of the murders of Abner and Amasa. Both had been victims of Joab's intense jealousy.

10. Merrill F. Unger, "Joab," in *Unger's Bible Dictionary,* p. 592.

Abner's murder was in revenge for the death of Joab's brother, Asahel, whom Abner killed in self-defense (2 Sam 2:12—3:1). Abner, who had risen to a place of great political prestige in Saul's kingdom, defected to Ish-bosheth. He later visited David. As Abner returned to tell his troops that they should accept David's regency, he was followed by some of Joab's men and forced to return to Hebron. At the gate of the city, Joab killed him (2 Sam 3:22-27). David's response at the time was twofold. He declared his innocence in the action and pronounced a curse upon the "head of Joab and on all his father's house" (2 Sam 3:29).

The second victim, Amasa, had commanded Absalom's forces. Because of Joab's disobedience in killing Absalom, David turned over to Amasa the command of the army. Following Absalom's death, David had to face the problem of political maneuvering between the ten northern tribes and the men of Judah (2 Sam 19:40-43). One of the complainers was Sheba, whom *The Living Bible* describes as a "hothead." He persuaded a significant number of the northerners to withdraw their loyalty from David. Alarmed at Sheba's revolt and its far-reaching implications, David decided to "nip it in the bud." He commissioned Amasa to have troops readied within three days. Amasa was evidently frustrated in his attempts, probably because the troops distrusted him—a factor David should have considered before elevating him to the high military post. Impatient with Amasa's delay, David sent his own troops under the command of Abishai. Forces still loyal to Joab followed his lead and marched with Abishai. At Gibeon, long known for its association with the Benjamites, Amasa caught up with them. Feigning friendship, Joab embraced Amasa, and, with a thrust of his short sword into the abdomen, Joab killed his replacement (2 Sam 20:4-10).

In his charge to Solomon, David as leader took the responsibility for Joab's crimes. He described the crimes as those that "Joab . . . did to me" (2:5). This blood must be avenged, and the matter of vengeance had been brought to a point of decision by Joab's uniting with the treachery of Adonijah. David's instructions regarding Joab were simply that he was not to die in peace.

Next, David mentioned Barzillai. He was remembered because he showed hospitality to David when the king was fleeing from Absalom into exile east of the Jordan. His kindnesses are briefly recounted in 2 Samuel 17:27-29. As David was returning to Jerusalem, he offered Barzillai a place in his court. This the aged Gileadite declined, but recommended his son Chimham for the position. David was essentially commanding Solomon to provide for the members of this loyal family.

The last person to be mentioned was Shimei, who first appeared in Scripture in a rather pitiful scene. The rebellion of Absalom had deeply wounded David. Shimei had added to those injuries by cursing the king and throwing stones at him and his followers as they passed the village of Bahurim (2 Sam 16:5-14). As a member of Saul's family, Shimei felt that David was responsible for the death of his kinsman. Shimei's acts seemingly would have brought retaliation, but David's sense of justice spared him. As David returned from exile, Shimei, with a great display of apology, met the victors at Gilgal. David spared his life, probably because of the victorious celebration (2 Sam 19:22). But the curse Shimei had uttered still hung like a storm cloud in David's memory, and now Shimei's punishment was ordered.

### DAVID'S DEATH
### 1 Kings 2:10-12

David died and was buried in the city that his forces had conquered, and that had become the central place of power for the unified nation. The tomb of David shown to tourists today presents a problem of identification. The site is located on the western hill of Jerusalem, but David's fortress never included that section. Many believe that the real burial vault is located somewhere at the southern end of the southeastern hill called Ophel.

David's forty-year reign was marked with great success and great failure. He was a military genius. He forged out victories that extended not only the nation's borders but its influence as well. At the end of his reign, all the elements of insurrection lifted their heads. Those elements were subdued, but they provided an ominous climate for the future. For the time being, however, Solomon's succession was unchallenged, and he ruled a united nation.

# 2

## Solomon in All His Glory

### 1 Kings 2:13—11:43

Many characters in Scripture command attention and are well known for the good and the bad they did. Adam and Eve are notorious for their sin, Methulselah for his great age, Noah for building the ark, Moses for the Red Sea crossing and receiving the Law, and David for his victory over Goliath. Solomon is remembered for his wisdom.

The biblical account of Solomon is scanty. Including the material in 2 Chronicles, his exploits are recorded in about twenty chapters. Compared to David, he comes off poorly. He is a distant finisher to Saul as well, especially when one considers that almost half of the twenty chapters do not concern Solomon at all, but the Temple that he was privileged to build. Indeed, it was the Temple's importance that probably gave importance to Solomon, and not the other way around.

The content of 2 Chronicles 1-8 is pertinent to the account in 1 Kings. As in the chronicler's portrayal of David, no mention is made of any impiety or weakness in Solomon's character. In a sense, 2 Chronicles resembles the evaluation that a loving, heavenly Father makes of believers. "There is therefore now no condemnation for those who are in Christ Jesus" (Rom 8:1). The historians responsible for 1 Kings, however, recorded his exploits "warts and all."

Some have been very hard on Solomon. These have noted his seeming inhumanity and apostasy. Scroggie, for instance, mentions only four righteous acts of Solomon and expresses some doubt about one of them. Then he listed nine negative episodes which cause him to see Solomon as a ruler resembling his predecessor Saul.[1] Others have treated Solomon with more kindness, noting, in all candor, his spiritual declension at the end of his reign.

Little has been revealed of Solomon's forty-year reign from 970-931 B.C. What is told in Scripture is a collage of greatness. The record in 1 Kings can be arranged into four divisions as the chart on pages 60-61 indicates: the organization of Solomon's kingdom, the building of the Temple, the wealth and fame of Solomon, and the apostasy of Solomon.

## THE ESTABLISHMENT OF POWER

### 1 Kings 2:13—4:34

Solomon was victorious over Adonijah's attempt to seize the throne, and had undoubtedly passed the mourning period over his father's death. In this section, which concerns the early Solomonic era, he was an untested monarch; but the tests came quickly.

The first test had to do with his father's enemies. David had exacted certain promises from Solomon concerning individuals, and these individuals all posed certain threats to Solomon's rule. So the first test related to the establishment of Solomon as the unchallenged king of Israel.

Five individuals figure prominently in this section. The first was innocent, but the others threatened the security of his throne. The five were Abishag, the Shunammite (cf. 1:2-4); Adonijah, the half-brother of Solomon and defeated usurper of power; Abiathar, the high priest who aided Adonijah; Joab, the general

1. William G. Scroggie, *The Unfolding Drama of Redemption,* 1:270-71.

whose conspiracy almost succeeded in bringing Adonijah to the throne; and Shimei, Saul's relative who had cursed David (2:8-9).

## ADONIJAH AND ABISHAG (2:13-25)

Some have suggested that Abishag was a partner in Adonijah's request. Scripture does not indicate that she was at all involved. To the western mind, Adonijah's petition probably does not seem too extreme. He had, however, represented a threat to Solomon and evidently still had a contingent of supporters among the people. Abishag belonged to the king's harem; an attempt to raid that harem might have been understood as an attack on the throne itself. Whether this was in Adonijah's mind when he enlisted Bathsheba's support is not known. But Solomon reacted as if this were the case. He felt that to ask for Abishag for a wife was tantamount to asking for the kingdom (2:22). This verse demonstrate's Solomon's sensitivity regarding his elevation to the throne. The age of his brother and the possible conspiracy of Abiathar and Joab could be countered only by strong measures. Solomon commissioned Benaiah, who was to become captain of the guard, and Benaiah killed Adonijah.

## ABIATHAR, THE PRIEST (2:26-27)

The second conspirator to be dealt with was the priest who, though faithful to David, had supported Adonijah as his successor. Solomon's treatment of the priest was mitigated because of the sacred office he held, and because he had been loyal to David. Abiathar, however, was removed from the priestly office and banished to Anathoth, a small town about three miles northeast of Jerusalem. Verse 27 may indicate that mercy was shown to him because he was evidently the sole survivor of Eli's family. The writer explains Abiathar's exile as a part of the judgment spoken earlier (see 1 Sam 2:27-30).

## JOAB, THE GENERAL (2:28-35)

Recalling Joab's murder of both Abner and Amasa, David had commanded Solomon to make sure that Joab died violently. In addition, Solomon knew Joab had supported Adonijah in the unsuccessful coup. And probably Joab was behind Adonijah's request to marry Abishag and was therefore also culpable for that.

After Adonijah's death and the order for Abiathar's exile, Joab fled the palace of worship and grabbed the horns of the altar. Adonijah had done the same thing earlier (1:50). The altar had been instituted as a place of safety, but only for one whose crime was accidental. Otherwise, the Scripture declared, "You shall take him from my altar that he may die" (Exod 21:14). Benaiah, upon orders from the king, went to the altar and there killed him. The body of this once valiant soldier was laid to rest in his family tomb, and David's words, "Let not his hoar head go down to the grave in peace" (2:6, KJV), were fulfilled. Abiathar's and Joab's vacant positions were filled by Zadok and Benaiah.

## SHIMEI, THE CURSER (2:36-46)

Throwing rocks and cursing, Shimei appeared in Scripture for the first time as David and his army were fleeing from Absalom. Shimei's life was supported by a thin thread as David's men wished to kill him on the spot (2 Sam 16:5-13). Shimei was not pardoned—his execution was merely delayed. As in the case of Joab, David commanded Solomon to bring Shimei to a violent end.

Solomon first employed a penalty similar to that imposed upon Abiathar. Shimei was made a prisoner of the city of Jerusalem. He was forbidden to leave its environs—the Kidron Valley on the east was the extent of freedom. Saul's kinsman agreed to this condition, and for three years the arrangement worked satisfactorily.

Evidently the arrangement regarding Shimei was not secret, at least not from his slaves. No doubt they felt immunity from either pursuit or penalty if they ran away. One day two of them ran off to the city of Gath in Philistia. Shimei was not to be deprived of his property. When he learned where they were, he too headed for Gath. This was the opportunity Solomon had sought; Shimei had disobeyed and, despite the circumstances, he too was killed.

SUMMARY

Solomon's acts seem vindictive. He may appear almost inhumane, and one wonders why he did not allow God to dispose of his enemies in His own good time and in His own ways. Again, it is well to remind oneself that this is not a panorama of western society. Each of the men who were executed had been a part of a plot, a rival faction, and still posed a possible threat to the new king. The writer of Kings notes why this section is important as he concludes, "And the kingdom was established in the hand of Solomon" (2:46).

## THE ENDOWMENT OF WISDOM
### 1 Kings 3:1-28

THE MARRIAGE OF SOLOMON (3:1)

"Then Solomon formed a marriage alliance with Pharaoh king of Egypt, and took Pharaoh's daughter and brought her to the city of David" (3:1). Solomon's marriage was probably a means of sealing an alliance with Pharaoh Siamon of the twenty-first dynasty.[2] Since Egyptian princesses were not usually sent to foreign countries, Solomon's marriage to the princess therefore shows his importance.

But verse 1 seems strangely out of place in the third chapter of 1 Kings. For that reason, some question whether it belongs here or should appear in chapter 9 where reference is made to Pharaoh's daughter being given to Solomon. Possibly the best

2. Jack P. Lewis, *Historical Backgrounds of Bible History,* pp. 16-17.

solution, suggested by the Codex Alexandrinus of the Septuagint as well as other authorities, is to connect this verse with the last phrase of chapter 2. In fact, 1 Kings 3:1-3 could easily be linked with the last sentence of 2:46 as describing the situation in Israel at the beginning of Solomon's reign.

### THE WORSHIP OF JEHOVAH (3:2-4)

From the time the Israelite's arrived in Canaan, the central place of worship had shifted from one location to another. The "high places" were undoubtedly places where the people of Israel worshiped Jehovah. Jamieson points out that these had become identified with idolatry because of their use by the patriarchs. The high places were venerated places. As such, they were forbidden to the people of Israel (Lev 17:3-4). Jamieson adds:

> But as long as the tabernacle was migratory, and the means for the national worship were merely provisional, the worship on those high places was tolerated; and hence, as accounting for their continuance, it is expressly stated (v. 2) that God had not yet chosen a permanent and exclusive place for His worship.[3]

So, Solomon went to one of these places of worship at Gibeon to make sacrifice. The fact that the king selected Gibeon as distinct from all other "high places" gave that location an interim importance as the principal place of worship. There the tent of meeting, the brazen altar, and the priestly intercession for the Israelites was to be conducted.

### THE VISION OF SOLOMON AND BESTOWAL OF WISDOM (3:5-15)

Solomon's dream at Gibeon was no ordinary dream. It was visionlike, for in it Solomon had opportunity to converse with God. Part of the Old Testament's means of revelation was through such visions, and, except for Isaiah's account of a

3. Robert Jamieson, "Joshua-Esther," in *A Commentary, Critical, Experimental and Practical on the Old and New Testaments,* by Robert Jamieson, A. R. Fausset, and David Brown, 2:310.

heavenly scene (Isa 6), this was the last recorded one until the time of Ezekiel and Daniel.

Jehovah appeared to Solomon and said, "Ask what I shall give you" (3:5, author's trans.). Recognizing his own weaknesses and realizing that money and honor cannot provide the acumen necessary for ruling, Solomon asked for "an understanding heart to judge Thy people" (3:9). Solomon did not ask for general wisdom but for that which specifically refers to the governance of his kingdom. "It reflects one aspect of his administration for which we have no record, that is, the organization of the law of his realm."[4]

"And the speech pleased the Lord" (3:10, KJV). Solomon had asked for the most important quality a ruler needs. The biblical concept of rule is one in which administration of justice avenges wrongdoing and rewards the right. Solomon sought the most necessary thing, and God rewarded him with much more. Solomon would be renowned for wisdom and for the grandeur of his kingdom. His name would command respect, and his rule would be lengthy.

## THE DEMONSTRATION OF THE UNDERSTANDING HEART (3:16-28)

Matters of justice are not always easily solved. Anyone who has experienced the rivalries of children is aware that the instigators of difficulty occasionally go unpunished. Every situation is not clear-cut. To separate truth from falsehood is often difficult. The understanding of Solomon was now tested.

Two prostitutes appeared before him. Both of them were contending for one child, and each was vehemently persuasive that the child was her own. Both women had recently delivered infants, and one of the infants had died. One woman was obviously lying, but which one? Solomon's solution was to provoke a demonstration of maternal love. His order to cut the child in half

4. James A. Montgomery, *A Critical and Exegetical Commentary on the Books of Kings*, p. 107.

brought the immediate response from the real mother, "Oh, my
lord, give her the living child, and in no wise slay it" (1 Kings
3:26, KJV). The other woman agreed to the command. Thus
the dispute was resolved, and Solomon's wisdom verified.

### THE ORGANIZATION OF THE KINGDOM

### 1 Kings 4:1-34

The delegation of responsibility is a mark of "wisdom." The
Solomonic kingdom was well ordered. In direct contact with the
king were ten chief officers ("princes," KJV). The kingdom
itself was divided into twelve districts, each governed by an
overseer.

#### THE CHIEF OFFICERS (4:1-6)

The ten chief officers advised the king. At the top of the list
was Azariah, the son of Zadok. Some commentators have suggested that he occupied a position of prime minister.[5] Others
have contended that he was the high priest.[6] Another view is
suggested by Montgomery and Gehman. Their argument stems
from the proper name that begins verse 3, Elihoreph. The name
literally means *God of autumn.* Since autumn was the beginning
of the calendar year, this officer ranked as the "Officer-Over-the-
Year" and was paralleled in the Roman court by the Pontifex
Maximus.[7]

The second office in the state was that of scribe and, accepting
the traditional view, two occupied this position, Elihoreph and
Ahijah. The office of scribe was comparable to our secretary of
state. This office prepared royal edicts—edicts that affected trade,
military alliances, and general commerce.

The royal recorder, Jehoshaphat, was responsible for main-

5. C. F. Keil and Franz Delitzsch, *Biblical Commentary on the Old Testament,*
   vol. 6, *The Books of the Kings,* by C. F. Keil, p. 44.
6. Jamieson, p. 302.
7. Montgomery, pp. 113-16.

taining a daily account of events pertaining to the kingdom. Jehoshaphat had held this office under David and continued under Solomon (see 2 Sam 8:16; 20:24).

Benaiah was prominent in these early events, and as head of the military, he commanded both prestige and power. His loyalty to the king was demonstratedly unflinching.

The naming of Abaithar—disposed as he was to Anathoth—and Zadok presents a difficulty. Theodoret's suggestion is probably correct—Solomon had deprived Abiathar of the high priestly office, but he retained the dignity of priest since this was hereditary.[8]

Azariah's and Zabud's link with the name *Nathan* leads to some confusion. Two Nathans were contemporaries. One was the prophet, and the other was a son of David (2 Sam 5:14). There is disagreement over which was referred to. Unger states that Nathan the son of David "appears to have taken no part in the events of his father's or his brother's reigns." Of the prophet, Nathan's son, he states: "His son Zabud succeeded him as the 'king's friend,' and another son, Azariah, was over the offices 'in Solomon's time.' "[9] On the other hand, Keil insists that both Azariah and Zabud were Solomon's nephews.[10]

Zabud was a confidential advisor to the king, and this fact possibly lends evidence to his (and his brother's) descent from the prophet Nathan. If not, there was a strange silence in the court about a prophetic figure. Thus it is possible that Zabud brought the prophetic element into the kingdom, though it must be understood that Zabud is nowhere spoken of as a prophet. A further complication is indicated by some translations that identify Zabud as a priest to Solomon.* This would eliminate Zabud as a mem-

8. Keil, p. 45.
9. Merrill F. Unger, *Unger's Bible Commentary*, p. 777.
10. Keil, p. 45.
    *1 Kings 4:5; translation, *New American Standard Bible;* paraphrase, *The Living Bible.*

ber of the Davidic family and cause confusion because Nathan the prophet was never said to have been from a priestly family. Though the problem of identity may not be solved, two explanations are possible: (1) Zabud and Azariah may have been the sons of neither of the Nathans prominent in this chronicle but of yet another one. (2) The word "priest" could be taken to mean *official*.

### THE TWELVE PREFECTURAL OFFICERS (4:7-19)

Twelve prefectural officers supervised the geographical areas from which Solomon received provisions. Each territory was responsible for provisions for a month. It is easy to assume that there was a sigh of relief when the days of obligation ended, for the daily provisions for the court were staggering: "And Solomon's provision for one day was thirty kors [195 bushels] of fine flour and sixty kors [390 bushels] of meal, ten fat oxen, twenty pasture-fed oxen, a hundred sheep besides deer, gazelles, roebucks, and fattened fowl" (1 Kings 4:22-23).

### THE STATE OF THE KINGDOM (4:20-34)

Solomon's kingdom was marked by national unity, security, and personal prosperity. The nation's strength resulted from Solomon's dedication to God and provision for national defense. The reference to forty thousand chariot horses (v. 26) should probably be four thousand as 2 Chronicles 9:25 indicates. This is also in better agreement with the number of charioteers available.

Solomon was a multigifted regent. Beside his administrative abilities, he demonstrated that he was a man of the arts; being a poet, lyricist, and student of life sciences made him more than a mere well-rounded individual.

## The Building of the Temple

### 1 Kings 5:1—6:38

#### THE PREPARATION (5:1-18)

To the north lay the friendly country of Tyre. Its king, Hiram, had been an old friend to David. Seemingly this amicable relationship between the two countries continued uninterrupted when Solomon ascended the throne. The land of the kingdom of Tyre is today marked by the beauty and magnificence of two mountain ranges. On their slopes, in Solomon's day, rose the forests of cedars with which he wished to build much of the Temple of Jehovah. Hiram was contracted to supply lumber and servants. The agreement included transportation. The logs were to be bound into rafts and then floated down to Israel.

In addition to the Lebanese laborers, Solomon drafted thirty thousand from Israel. These worked in Lebanon in three shifts, allowing one month at work and two at home. Seventy thousand more were charged with the delivery of materials. Another eighty thousand were masons hewing stones. Thus, in addition to the Lebanese work force, Israel supplied almost two hundred thousand workers to this project. The Temple was no "cost-efficiency," budget-cutting project!

#### THE PROJECT (6:1-38)

The author begins the account in chapter 6 with a chronology. The building was begun in the fourth year of Solomon's reign, 480 years after the Exodus. This reference is important for dating purposes. Solomon's reign began about 971 B.C., and is an excellent biblical argument for 1440 B.C. as the approximate date of the Exodus.

A description of the Temple follows. The main sanctuary building, unpretentious as to dimensions, was thirty feet wide, ninety feet long, and forty-five feet high. In terms of square footage, the Temple was about the size of a large home. The importance of the building lay not in massiveness.

Although the size was conservative, the decor of the Temple was not. The use of gold and silver as well as the magnificence of cedar wood provided an awesome sight. The exterior of the Temple was white limestone, much of which was quarried in deposits that are now beneath the northern wall of the Old City. In Solomon's time the deposits were quarried north of the Davidic city. The Temple's magnificence was further amplified by the number of workmen who labored there, as well as the seven and one-half years required to build it.

The importance of the Temple dare not be minimized. This structure, and the attitude of Solomon's heirs toward it, formed the basis of evaluation of their reigns as recorded in 1 and 2 Chronicles. And the prominence of the Temple (though not Solomon's) is often referred to in the New Testament.

## SOLOMON'S RESIDENCE
### 1 Kings 7:1-8

These few verses, which seem strangely placed, intimate that Solomon had three separate residences. Most commentators concede that the first house was his royal palace in the city of Jerusalem. The thirteen years of building do not indicate that more time, and consequently more ornamentation, were lavished on his house than on the Temple. Rather, great time-consuming preparations were not made for it as for the Temple, and neither was there need for haste in its construction.

The reference to "the house of the forest of Lebanon" (v. 2) presents a minor problem. Is this a separate residence from that mentioned in verse 1 or does the phrase mean that Solomon's house in Jerusalem, being constructed of Lebanese cedar wood, was dubbed with that title? Was the author of 1 Kings emphasizing the residence's predominant decor rather than its location? Some writers have conjectured that this was a separate palace from that in verse 1. Further references however indicate this building was a part of a great royal complex consisting of the royal residence, the great hall and armory, and the residence for the Egyptian princess, Solomon's bride.

The floor plan of the palace area was similar to other Eastern royal houses. The dominant feature was the hall of pillars (v. 6). Measuring forty-five feet by seventy-five feet, this room probably housed the three hundred golden shields (see 1 Kings 10:17) and served as an armory (see Isa 22:8).

The palace had also a tribunal hall (v. 7), or a place of judgment, and a separate residence for the queen. Jamieson summed up these verses:

> This arrangement of the palace accords with the Oriental style of building, according to which a great mansion always consists of three divisions or separate houses, all connected by doors and passages—the men dwelling at one extremity, the female portion of the family at the other, while public rooms occupy the central part of the building.[11]

## THE TEMPLE FURNISHINGS

### 1 Kings 7:9-51

THE STONEWORK (7:9-12)

No doubt the writer of 1 Kings desired to discuss both major building projects in Jerusalem, but of these the Temple was not only more magnificent but of far greater importance. The significant point made about the stonework was the immensity of the individual stones. Sizes of fifteen and twelve feet seem to the uninformed reader too large for ancient times. However, great stones are found in many ancient edifices—the pyramids and funeral palaces of Egypt, and the Greek temples, to name a few. The limestone of Palestine can be sawed when newly quarried, and it hardens with further exposure to the elements.[12]

11. Jamieson, p. 310.
12. John Gray, *I and II Kings*, p. 181.

THE CRAFTSMANSHIP OF HIRAM (7:13-47)

Two persons bore the name Hiram in Solomonic history. The first, of course, was the king of Tyre mentioned in 5:1. The second was an Israelite of the tribe of Naphtali. To add to the confusion, he also came from Tyre. The two were distinguished, however, by their job descriptions. The king of Tyre gave orders, wrote edicts, and cared for the matters of state involved in the Solomonic enterprise, whereas The other Hiram was involved with the craftsmanship of the bronze work and the furnishings of the Temple.

The description of the bronze work of the Temple makes apparent that great quantities of the metal were used. Nelson Glueck, the distinguished Israeli archaeologist, discovered mines belonging to this period in the Jordan area as well as south of the Dead Sea.

> Nelson Glueck found a great deal of evidence to show that the mines in this area were worked from about the days of David onward for several centuries. But the activity was particularly intense in the days of Solomon. Quite apart from the many small furnaces found in the area below the Dead Sea, Glueck was able to excavate the ancient site of Ezion Geber. Here he found that a flourishing town existed in the days of Solomon. The most important discovery was that this town was a center of copper refining. An amazing building was uncovered in which the ancient crucibles were still to be seen in place. The smelting was carried out by making use of the strong winds blowing from the north. Draughts were led into the furnaces, and the refining process was carried out in a highly technical manner.[13]

Although recent scholarship takes the view that Solomon's mines were located elsewhere, the account of Glueck's findings is enlightening. It reveals the point to which copper refining had developed in this period.

13. J. A. Thompson, *The Bible and Archaeology*, pp. 105-6.

Mention of the articles Hiram crafted begins with a description of the two bronze pillars that were placed on the porch, one on each side of the entrance doors. The choice of their names, Jachin and Boaz, is significant. Gehman presents an interesting discussion of the evolution of the names and concludes, with a number of other scholars, that the two names form a kind of cryptogram for "In the strength of YHWH shall the king rejoice."[14]

The bronze sea is described next. Probably the replacement of the bronze laver of the Tabernacle, this pool was much larger. It measured fifteen feet in diameter and stood well over seven feet high. Supported on twelve bronze oxen, three to a side, the sea was an imposing sight in the Temple courtyard. The water in the bronze sea was probably the source of water for the portable basins described in 7:27-38. It should be noted that these were no easily wheeled carriages to be moved about by a couple of priests. Their size as well as the combined weight of metal and water bring estimates of their weight to well over a ton. The height of stands and basins, approximately seven and one-half feet, would necessitate some means of ascent to the lavers or a means of dispensing the water at the bottom. Smaller furnishings are mentioned in an apparent recapitulation of the work of Hiram of Tyre in verses 40-47.

### THE GOLD ARTICLES (7:48-50)

The writer does not share the detail of the articles fashioned of gold. But these were the inner furnishings, whereas the bronze were those outside.

### THE INVENTORY OF WEALTH (7:51)

So the work was completed. The recorder passes quickly over the inventory of wealth, which comprised not only the utensils and furnishings of the house of worship but also the contents of the treasury.

14. Montgomery, p. 171.

## THE DEDICATION OF THE TEMPLE

### 1 Kings 8:1-66

Chapter 8 furnishes a climax to the first section of 1 Kings. The Temple dedication climaxed Solomon's accomplishments insofar as God was concerned. This is especially evident in 2 Chronicles. Not only is no reference made to Solomon's apostasy, but each king following Solomon is evaluated on the basis of his service to God through the prescribed rituals.

The chapter is easily divided into four sections. The first recounts the period of "moving in" (vv. 1-21). The most important item to be moved was the one article of furniture from the wilderness tent of meeting that was not replaced—the Ark of the Covenant. Next came the magnificent dedicatory prayer by Solomon (vv. 22-53); the third section is Solomon's exhortation (vv. 54-61); and the chapter concludes with commands to the people and a fourteen-day feast (vv. 54-66).

#### THE TEMPLE FURNISHED (8:1-21)

The day of dedication finally arrived. Workers had labored seven years in its anticipation. Now a great convocation was scheduled for the seventh month of the year at the time of the Feast of Tabernacles. All of Israel's major and minor leaders were called to this solemn gathering. Nothing like this had been witnessed since the day the tabernacle had been consecrated (Exod 40). As the witnesses gathered, the priests began the procession that brought the earlier tabernacle and its furnishings to the new site. Many utensils for worship had been preserved from the tabernacle; with the exception of the Ark, all furnishings were replaced with newer and grander pieces.

The importance of the Ark is evident by the detail given concerning its carrying, the place in which it was to be located, and the mention of its contents. In addition, Solomon stated that the Temple was built with the Ark in mind (8:20-21). The description of the poles is interesting in that their length is mentioned. The fact that the poles were not removed indicates that the priests continued to obey the command of Exodus 25:15, "The poles shall remain in the rings of the ark; they shall not be removed from it."

Inside the Ark were the two stone tables on which were written the Ten Commandments (1 Kings 8:9). Keil comments that this reference was "simply to show that the law, which enjoined that the ark should merely preserve the stone tables of the covenant (Ex. xxv. 16; xl. 20), had not been departed from in the lapse of time."[15] (The book of Hebrews refers to Aaron's rod and to the manna as also being in the Ark [Heb 9:4]. This was true of the tabernacle to which he referred.) The significance is that the same covenant relationship established between Jehovah and the people of Israel, represented by both the Ark and the tables of stone, was to continue in the new setting.

When the priests came out of the building, an awesome phenomenon occurred. The cloud of the glory of the Lord filled the house (2 Chron 7:1-2). This visible symbol of God's presence confirmed to Solomon and the people that the Lord was pleased with the work. The same confirmatory evidence marked the dedication of the tabernacle (Exod 40:34-35). The cloud did not remain visible to the people. After the dedication, it was visible only to the high priest when he entered the Holy of Holies on the Day of Atonement.

Reading only the account in 1 Kings, one wonders that there was no expression of praise from the congregation. According to 2 Chronicles 5:12-13 there was

> all the Levitical singers, Asaph, Heman, Jeduthun, and their sons and kinsmen, clothed in fine linen, with cymbals, harps, and lyres, standing east of the altar, and with them one hundred and twenty priests blowing trumpets, in unison when the trumpeters and the singers were to make themselves heard with one voice to praise and to glorify the LORD, and when they had

15. Keil, p. 122.

lifted up their voice accompanied by trumpets and cymbals
and instruments of music, and when they praised the Lord
saying, "He indeed is good for His lovingkindness is everlast-
ing," then the house, the house of the Lord, was filled with a
cloud.

This fantastic spectacle reminded Solomon of the history of
the cloud phenomenon. He praised God and spoke of David's
purpose to build the sanctuary as a permanent place where Jehovah's name would be remembered.

### SOLOMON'S PRAYER OF DEDICATION (8:22-53)

Solomon seems to have moved to a place erected for praying
the prayer of dedication. He first stood beside the altar, and then
fell to his knees (cf. 8:54). The prayer is a model one. It began
as prayer should, not with requests but with worship.

### *Worshiping in prayer (8:23-29)*

Regarding prayer, our Lord said, "Pray, then, in this way: 'Our
Father who art in heaven, Hallowed be Thy name' " (Matt 6:9).
Solomon began in much the same spirit. He extolled the greatness
of God, and that was real worship. He described God's unique-
ness (v. 23), His faithfulness (vv. 24-26), His infinity (v. 27),
and His compassion and concern (vv. 28-29). Verse 27 is one
of the grand passages of Scripture denoting the infinity of God.
Many worshipers since Solomon have reflected on this attribute.
Augustine was one example as he cried out,

> And how shall I call upon my God, my God and Lord, since
> when I call for Him, I shall be calling Him to myself? and what
> room is there within me, whither my God can come into me?
> whither can God come into me, God who made heaven and
> earth? is there, indeed, O Lord my God, aught in me that can
> contain Thee? do then heaven and earth, which Thou hast
> made, and wherein Thou has made me, contain Thee?[16]

16. Augustine, *The Confessions of St. Augustine, Harvard Classics*, vol. 7,
p. 6.

*Interceding in prayer (8:30-53)*

The rest of the prayer related to varied and extensive requests. The key to Solomon's petitioning is probably verse 26: "Let Thy word, I pray Thee, be confirmed." To Solomon, Jehovah was a God who made specific and definite promises and fulfilled them. Solomon prayed for needs with confidence that those who sinned, those who were defeated, all those who had needs would bring their cares to the Temple. "This house" was central to the intercessory part of his prayer. Three different expressions for prayer in verse 28 also are instructive. The word translated "prayer" denotes prayer in general. The second word, "supplication," is a specific form of prayer, a call for help. The third, "cry," literally means "a ringing cry."

This prayer of Solomon anticipated the future of Israel. In verses 33 and 34, he requested that Israel's repentance would result in her release from captivity and return to the land. Sin was recognized as a cause of God's withholding His blessings (vv. 35, 38, 46). And Solomon acknowledged that the care of Israel was God's responsibility: "They are Thy people and Thine inheritance which Thou has brought forth from Egypt" (1: 51).

## SOLOMON'S EXHORTATION TO THE PEOPLE (8:54-61)

Rising from prayer, Solomon turned to face the people of Israel, blessed them, and reminded them of Jehovah's faithfulness in keeping His promises (vv. 54-56). Solomon then began a twofold request. He asked that Jehovah be present with them as He had been with their fathers, so that He could incline the hearts of the people toward Himself and His commandments (vv. 57-58). Then Solomon requested that the Lord be aware of his prayer day and night, and that He care for him and the people of Israel so the people of the world would know that "the LORD is God" (v. 60).

The statement, "the LORD is God," is almost a creedal statement. Gray calls it "the confession of faith," and Montgomery, "a battlecry."[17] This statement would appear later when Elijah faced the prophets of Baal on Mount Carmel (1 Kings 18:39).

Solomon exhorted the people to completely commit themselves to Jehovah on the basis of theological principle and practical desire. Such a commitment was to be active; it was to result in a life of obedience to God (v. 61). At this point "fire came down from heaven and consumed the burnt offering and the sacrifices; and the glory of the LORD filled the house" (2 Chron 7:1).

> Just as at the consecration of the Mosaic sanctuary the Lord did not merely manifest His gracious presence through the cloud which filled the tent, but also kindled the first sacrifice with fire from heaven (Lev. 9:24), to sanctify the altar as the legitimate place of sacrifice; so also at the temple, the miraculous kindling of the first sacrifice with fire from heaven was the immediate and even necesary consequence of the filling of the temple with the cloud, in which the presence of Jehovah was embodied.[18]

## THE GREAT FEAST (8:62-66)

This miraculous and awesome display from heaven was followed by a response of worship from the people. The large number of animal sacrifices has led some commentators to conclude that this is an error.[19] However, Keil points out that 250,000 lambs were slain in the time of Nero in a period of three hours. There were probably at least three thousand priests and a number of auxiliary altars.[20]

Solomon and the people of Israel worshiped and feasted for fourteen days. On the fifteenth day following the dedication, they returned to their tents "joyful and glad of heart for all the good-

17. Gray, p. 231; Montgomery, p. 199.
18. Keil, p. 134.
19. Montgomery, pp. 199-200.
20. Keil, p. 136.

ness that the LORD had shown to David His servant and to Israel His people" (v. 66).

## SOLOMON'S WEALTH, GLORY, AND HONOR

### 1 Kings 9—10

In a sense, Solomon's life was divided into two parts. The words that open chapter 9 mark the beginning of the second half of his forty-year reign. This period began with another appearance of the Lord to Solomon.

The nation had reached a high point. A magnificent center of worship had been completed, national prestige had never been higher, and the grandeur of the Solomonic era was beginning to attract international notice. No situation could have been more conducive to decay. Someone has commented that individuals and society go through the same stages. Both experience birth, infancy, childhood, adolescence, and robust adulthood, followed by deterioration and old age. The Solomonic society was at its robust best in chapters 9 and 10.

### JEHOVAH'S SECOND APPEARANCE (9:1-9)

Solomon's desires for his kingdom had been realized. The house of the Lord and the house of the king were no longer sketches on planning boards but beautiful, functional buildings. Now the drive that had motivated the king and his subjects for twenty years was in danger of becoming inert.

The Lord appeared to Solomon the second time with encouragement and warning. He began by acknowledging Solomon's faithfulness, and reiterated the fact that He was present in the Temple. He promised Solomon a perpetual throne as He had previously promised David (vv. 4-5). But fulfillment was conditioned upon the faithfulness of Solomon and his posterity. Failure to follow Him, Jehovah stated, would result in dispersion of the nation and destruction of the Temple (vv. 6-9). Not only would the effect upon the people of Israel be devastating, but the testimony of the Lord would be affected. One of the great lessons to be learned and not necessarily experienced is that God does deal with sin.

## THE COMMERCE AND LIFE OF THE SOLOMONIC EMPIRE (9:10-28)

### *The acquisition of gold (9:10-14)*

Again the king of Tyre, Hiram, appears in the account. He had furnished building materials as well as skilled laborers for Solomon. In this passage it appears that Hiram was paid by being given twenty cities in Galilee. It should be noted, however, that these cities were not payment for services rendered. Solomon paid Hiram for materials and men with wheat and oil (cf. 5:11). In fact, he sold the cities to Hiram for 120 talents of gold. Solomon wanted gold. The cities were probably small villages, and to Hiram were not particularly desirable. Solomon and Hiram may have struck a bargain, and the result of the bargain was the payment to Solomon.

The price of 120 talents is meaningless to most present-day people. There were two different measurements for a talent. The Babylonian talent was the equivalent of 130 pounds. The Jewish talent, which came later, weighed about 66 pounds. In contemporary terms, Hiram paid Solomon either $35 million (Babylonian scale) or $19 million (Jewish scale) for the twenty cities. Payment was in the king of metals—gold.

### *The labor force (9:15-22)*

In verses 15-22 we see the extent of Solomon's building enterprise. In a sense, Solomon and Herod the Great share the stage as great builders in Palestinian history. In addition to the Temple and the palace, the account speaks of a citadel (Millo), the city wall, plus three cities. *Millo* comes from a word that can refer to fill-in earthworks, terraces, embankments, or walls. In 2 Chronicles 32:5, the Septuagint speaks of the *Millo* as *analēmma* ("raised work"). Gray's opinion is that the "Millo" then consisted of the " 'filling' of the gulf between the City of David on the south-east hill and the Ophel, or 'bulge' to the northeast."[21]

The extension of fortifications for Jerusalem was necessitated by the completed Temple and palace which were to the north of the old City of David. The three fortress cities, Hazor, Megiddo, and Gezer were each strategically important. Hazor protected the northern routes into Galilee. Megiddo protected the fertile valley of Jezreel, and Gezer guarded the southern routes into the heartland of Solomon's kingdom.

Archaeology has revealed the excavated gateways of these three cities to have been the work of the same Solomonic architect.[22] Of these three, Gezer was singled out as a city having political implications for Solomon. Captured by an unnamed Egyptian pharaoh, it became a dowry for Solomon's wife.

Construction enterprises such as these required a great work force, and this was supplied by slaves who were remnants of the Canaanite groups that had occupied the land prior to the Israelite conquest. That the chronicler was not far removed from the events he recorded is evidenced by his reference "even to this day" (v. 21) concerning the slave force. He also pointed out that no Israelite was a member of the slave force that built the cities.

*The consolidation of the kingdom (9:23-28)*

Not offering a strict chronology, the writer mentions four additional items that reinforce the theme of this section, consolidation of the empire. First, Solomon's work force was supervised by 550 Israelites. The king's wisdom is once more apparent; he recognized that the Israelites would show more concern over the quality of work than the dispossessed Canaanites.

Second, the writer noted that the Millo was built after the pharaoh's daughter came to her palace in Jerusalem. The sig-

21. Gray, pp. 243-44.
22. Ibid., p. 246.

nificance of the reference is related again to the work to which the
slave force had been commissioned.

Third, Solomon's devotion to God was cited. Three times in
the same year Solomon offered sacrifices. These three times were
probably the Feast of Unleavened Bread, the Feast of Weeks, and
the Feast of Tabernacles.

And last, Solomon's merchant fleet was mentioned. Little detail was given. The port city was near the present Israeli port
Elath. The Phoenician sailors Hiram furnished to Solomon were
the finest seamen of their time. The fleet brought King Solomon
420 talents of gold—an awesome amount.

### THE VISIT OF THE QUEEN OF SHEBA (10:1-13)

Wealth and rapid growth were not the only significant happen-
ings in the Solomonic kingdom. Solomon's wisdom also captured notice. Apparently his wisdom was considered to be divinely ordained, and as such attracted the queen of Sheba.

Sheba is to be identified with modern Yemen. Solomon's mer-
cantile navy, operating along the Arabian coast, would have had
contact with this the most prosperous and important of the
Arabian kingdoms.

We are probably correct to conclude that the queen made the
fourteen-hundred-mile journey to Solomon's capital to do more
than "test him with difficult questions" (v. 1). Trade agreements
and some kind of political alliance were probably a part of the
agenda for her visit. But the test of difficult questions was important. If Solomon were divinely gifted with wisdom, he would
be able to solve all kinds of perplexing problems. That Solomon's
answers were more than satisfactory is evidenced in verse 3: he
"answered all her questions; nothing was hidden from the king
which he did not explain to her" (v. 3).

Verses 4 and 5 picture the queen as a very careful and ob-
servant person. This prompted Montgomery to comment that

the record "delineates the womanly observation of details."[23] The queen then expressed her reaction to what she had seen. She spoke of her skepticism of the reports that she had received and said, "The half was not told me." She marveled at the privileged position of the king's servants who continually drank of his wisdom. Then she extolled Solomon's God, who was the source of all that Solomon possessed. Finally, she presented expensive gifts to the king.

The almug trees, which comprised part of the cargo of the Solomonic fleet, were used for the Temple steps (2 Chron 9:11). This stairway was one of the things the queen had observed (v. 5). Further information concerning almug trees occurs in verses 11 and 12, where mention is made of almug instruments associated with the Temple music program.

The king presented gifts to the queen as well. The exchange of gifts, part of normal diplomatic protocol, is alluded to in the expression, "what he gave her according to his royal bounty" (v. 13). But Solomon did more: he gave her "all her desire" (v. 13). His response to this foreign queen pictures well the grace of God in His dealings with men. He not only supplies what is necessary, but "much more" (cf. Rom 5:15, 17, 20).

A SUMMARY OF SOLOMON'S WEALTH (10:14-29)

*His holdings in gold (10:14-22)*

Comment was made earlier concerning Solomon's accumulation of gold. Here the writer records that his receipt of gold in one year was equivalent to over $67 million. In reading the account, one must be impressed with the fact that gold was abundant throughout the royal buildings as well as in the Temple. The wry comment of verse 21 concerning silver as not being considered valuable in Solomon's kingdom must cause a modern reader to raise his eyebrows. And not only gold was imported,

23. Montgomery, p. 216.

but silver and ivory, and exotic pets such as apes and peacocks.

### *His international influence (10:23-25)*

The two marks of this man, riches and wisdom, continued to draw a retinue of world travelers to Jerusalem. And as they came, the coffers of Solomon's wealth filled, overflowed into new coffers, and the cycle continued.

### *His military force (10:26-29)*

In Solomon's day, chariots were the most feared of all forces that could be assembled on a battlefield. The speed with which they moved, as well as the advanced weaponry used from their platforms, made them the armored divisions of the ancient world. The tank battles of the recent Yom Kippur War were modern-day counterparts to the ancient use of chariots.

Until Solomon's time, Israel's military force had consisted of infantry. Solomon modernized his army by introducing the use of chariots and placing chariot forces strategically throughout the land.

Solomon's kingdom represented the epitome of prosperity, but the high life did not realistically characterize Solomon's realm. Working as a cancer were deteriorating influences that would soon split the kingdom into two rival factions.

## SOLOMON'S APOSTASY AND DECLINE

### 1 Kings 11

Solomon's life ended in disaster. Riding the crest of power has plunged many complacent men into defeat. Solomon undoubtedly came to believe that his sagacity, power, and prestige would see him through any difficulty. Power attracts enemies, but external opposition did not threaten Solomon as did his internal difficulties. It was on these internal problems that the writer of Kings first focuses attention.

SOLOMON'S APOSTASY (11:1-13)

*The unlawful alliances (11:1-3)*

Strangely, there is seemingly complete silence concerning the Law of Moses throughout the history of the kings. Whenever it is mentioned, the reference is only general. But the Law had clearly prohibited foreign marriages (Deut 7:1-5). With the newness of the great worship center scarcely gone, declension set in because of indulgence in the very things God had exhorted His people not to do.

The original law of monogamy (Gen 1:26-27; 2:24-25) had long been disregarded. David had made many alliances by marrying for political expediency. Solomon followed in his steps. The heir to the throne, Rehoboam, was a son of an Ammonite wife. Quoting from the Law in Exodus 23 and 34, the chronicler notes the condemnation of associating with foreigners. The perplexing thing is that Solomon, as far as we know, was not countered on this by either prophet or priest.

*The unholy practices (11:4-8)*

In spite of the warning, "Solomon held fast to these in love" (v. 2), and the result was as had been predicted: "They will surely turn your heart away after their gods (v. 2). The first step in the direction of apostasy was *compromise,* and that fact was attested by the statement "His heart was not wholly devoted to the LORD his God" (v. 4).

Solomon was not involved in a rejection of the worship of Jehovah. He just included with it the worship of other deities forbidden by the first commandment: "You shall have no other gods before Me" (Exod 20:3). Solomon had begun to engage in an inclusive religion. Neglecting the singleness of worship prescribed by the commandment, he instituted a kind of ecumenism.

Three heathen gods were given prominence in the religious system promoted by the king. Ashtoreth, also known as Astarte, was associated with fertility rites and her worship undoubtedly included star worship as well. Milcom was known also as Molech. Molech worship was the national religion of the Ammonites. The rites involved the offering of human sacrifice. The third deity to be recognized was Chemosh, national god of Moab. To satisfy his wives, the king threw away every important blessing of God.

## The unhappy penalty (11:9-13)

As Solomon had been warned when Jehovah spoke to him, the kingdom was to be torn from him. The throne would be given to his "servant," and which servant was meant was soon stated. This action, however, would be delayed until Solomon was dead; his son was to experience the judgment, yet one tribe would remain for him. The reason for this last gracious act on the part of God was His love for David and His desire to protect the city of Jerusalem that He had claimed for His own.

### SOLOMON'S ENEMIES (11:14-40)

The second section of the chapter has to do with the way God would remove Solomon from the throne. Three men became thorns in Solomon's side and complicated his plans for his kingdom and its future.

## Hadad the Edomite (11:14-22)

Hadad's conflict with Solomon began early. The bitterness that existed was the result of a military campaign by David. Little is stated concerning his opposition to Solomon, but this royal heir of Edom left the security of Egypt's courts to become Solomon's foe.

## Rezon of Damascus (11:23-25)

Along with Hadad, Rezon no doubt was forced to pay tribute. Both were troublemakers in the empire. The nature of Rezon's opposition is not specified, and we know only that he was "an adversary to Israel all the days of Solomon" (v. 25).

| ORGANIZATION | | | | THE TEMPLE |
|---|---|---|---|---|
| Abishag<br>Adonijah<br>Abiathar<br>Joab<br>Shimei | Marriage<br>Worship<br>Vision<br>Endowment<br>Sacrifice<br>Demonstration | Cabinet<br>Provincial<br>Officers<br>Royal Table<br>Intellectual<br>Pursuits | Hiram<br>Contract<br>Conscription | The Building<br>and<br>Grounds of<br>the Temple |
| **2** | **3** | **4** | **5** | **6** |
| The<br>Kingdom<br>Established | Solomon's<br>Wisdom | Organization and Agreements | | Solomon's<br>Building<br>Program |
| Death and<br>Exile | Wisdom,<br>Riches, and<br>Honor | Wisdom, Understanding,<br>Broad Interests | | The Temple<br>and a House |

| | |
|---|---|
| CHARACTER<br><br>2:46—"The kingdom was established in the hands of Solomon."<br><br>3:3—"Solomon loved the LORD."<br><br>3:28—"They saw that the wisdom of God was in him, to administer justice." | DAILY NEEDS<br>195 Bushels of flour<br>390 Bushels of meal<br>10 Oxen<br>20 Cattle<br>100 Sheep plus wild game<br><br>MILITARY FORCE<br>4,000 horses (text)<br>12,000 horsemen<br><br>HIS ABILITIES<br>Wiser than all men<br>3,000 proverbs<br>1,005 songs<br>Knowledge of: Botany, Zoology |

| OF YAHWEH | | WEALTH AND FAME | | APOSTASY |
|---|---|---|---|---|
| Solomon's House The Furnishings for Worship | Ark Brought in Solomon's Prayer Solomon's Exhortation 14 Days of Sacrifice | Second Appearance of Yahweh Payment to Hiram Slave Labor Completion of Building Holy Days Merchant Navy | Queen of Sheba Imports Wealth and High Life Tribute GNP | Foreign Wives Foreign Gods Foreign Conflicts Death |
| **7** | **8** | **9** | **10** | **11** |
| Solomon's Building Program | Dedication Day | Solomon's Wealth, Glory, and Honor | | Solomon's Apostasy |
| The Temple and a House | Praise, Humility, and Exhortation | The High Life | | The Low Life |
| | IF'S<br>1) A man sins against his neighbor.<br>2) Smitten down because of enemy.<br>3) No rain.<br>4) Famine, etc.<br>5) Foreigner calls upon Thee.<br>6) We go to battle.<br>7) We sin against Thee. | | | THREE ENEMIES<br>1) Hadad, the Edomite<br>2) Rezon, of Damascus<br>3) Jeroboam, the Ephraimite |

*Jeroboam the Ephraimite (11:26-40)*

Solomon's greatest political threat was not from Edom or Syria, but from within. Jeroboam had commended himself as "a valiant warrior" and was evidently one of the 550 officers who supervised Solomon's labor force (cf. 9:23 and 11:28). The Lord had a special mission for Jeroboam, and that was revealed to him by Ahijah, the prophet from Shiloh. In a dramatic gesture, Ahijah ripped his cloak into twelve pieces. He then revealed that Solomon's kingdom would be ripped into pieces, and one tribe alone would be left to the Davidic line.

The ten pieces of new cloak in Jeroboam's hand were explained. He was to become king over the major portion of the realm. In verse 38, God offered to him the same conditions He had presented Solomon a number of years before. He was promised a perpetual kingdom like that which He was perpetuating for David. Jeroboam was told why the kingdom was being divided: "They have forsaken Me" (v. 33). Thus he was both informed and warned.

The news of this startling announcement evidently reached the king, and Jeroboam suddenly was added to the "most-wanted list" in Israel. He sought refuge in Egypt and there awaited the death of Solomon.

SOLOMON'S DEATH (11:41-43)

Although marked by a long reign and opulence beyond imagination, this great man's history ended in tragedy. Solomon's achievements were glorious and, in a sense, history has been kind to him. Little is said concerning his multiplicity of wives or his apostasy. His wisdom, his accomplishments, and his glory are still bywords today. The short sentences of this passage reflect the punctuality of death, its certainty, and the reminder that life moves on, as Rehoboam was elevated to the throne.

# 3

# Division, Hostility, and Consolidation

## 1 Kings 12:1—16:28

The historical setting of the period to be viewed is one of unrest, constant war, threats from other nations, partial revival, revolution, assassinations, and gross immorality. Except for strange-sounding names such as Nadab or Zimri, one might think this section to be an account of a twentieth-century national struggle. The events covered in 1 Kings 12 were those that preceded and, in some cases, led to Elijah's ministry in the Northern Kingdom of Israel. The record in 1 Kings moves back and forth across the borders of Israel and Judah, and traces the histories, however brief, of the leaders of the two nations.

As mentioned in the introductory chapter, the dating accepted for this period is varied, even among evangelical scholars. For example, Scroggie set the beginning date of the divided kingdom at 975 B.C.,[1] but Albright set it at 922.[2] I find the most satisfactory date is 931-30, propounded by Thiele.[3] The interested student would do well to study Thiele's work with regard to the chronology and its synchronization in this period.

From the lengthy accounts of the ministries of Elijah and Elisha, it is obvious that the writer of 1 Kings wished to accord special prominence to these men. The study before us in this

1. W. G. Scroggie, *The Unfolding Drama of Redemption,* 1:290.
2. W. F. Albright, *The Biblical Period from Abraham to Ezra,* p. 58.
3. Edwin R. Thiele, *The Mysterious Numbers of the Hebrew Kings,* pp. 53-54.

chapter embraces the first two dynasties in Israel, the seven-day rule of Zimri, and the accounts of three Judean kings.

## THE DISRUPTION OF THE KINGDOM AT SHECHEM

### 1 Kings 12:1-24

Shechem was one of the most important cities in the northern portion of the Davidic kingdom. Beautifully situated on the lower slopes of Mount Gerizim and Mount Ebal, Shechem had a long history of importance to the social and religious life of the Israelites. Visitors to the ancient site can almost hear echoes of the solemn litanies uttered there by the twelve tribes (Deut 27:12).

Shechem is also the site of Jacob's well, important to the traveler of biblical days and to travelers today. Joseph was buried there (Josh 24:32), and it was the locale of the pastures of Jacob's sons. To Shechem, Rehoboam traveled, expecting to assume the throne as regent over all Israel since he had recently been acclaimed king in Judah. Seemingly this was also the desire of the people.

### JEROBOAM'S RETURN FROM EGYPT (12:2-4)

Having sought refuge in Egypt because of Solomon's distrust (see 1 Kings 11:40), Jeroboam returned to lead the Israelites' cause against the high taxes and forced labor imposed by the new king's father. Hopefully, relaxation of Solomon's stern programs would mark the coronation of the new monarch. Jeroboam, representing the northern tribes, requested of Rehoboam, "Lighten the hard service of your father and his heavy yoke which he put on us, and we will serve you" (v. 4).

It is difficult to assess what really was going on in the mind of Jeroboam. He was fully aware of the prophecy of Ahijah. Was he playing a cat and mouse game that would provide opportunity for rebellion? In light of the context, it is more likely that, although Jeroboam was waiting for his opportunity to assume leadership, the northern tribes were still somewhat ambivalent about any change in the condition of a united kingdom.

### REHOBOAM'S COUNSEL AND DECISION (12:6-15)

Rehoboam asked for three days to make his decision concerning the people's request. He first consulted the elders. The term *elder* probably referred to both the mature age and the status of the leader. Elders were counselors who could draw from a large bank of experience and history. The elders told Rehoboam to do what the people had asked—be their servant. This way Rehoboam would receive their undying loyalty (v. 7).

"But he forsook the counsel of the elders" (v. 8). Rehoboam did not want to display any weakness. He felt he must fit his father's image. He turned to his peer group for counsel, and their counsel varied 180 degrees from that of the elders. They encouraged Rehoboam to display his might. At the end of three days, he went to the assembly and, following the advice of his younger friends; said, "My father made your yoke heavy, but I will add to your yoke; my father disciplined you with whips, but I will discipline you with scorpions" (v. 14). Concerning the term "scorpions," Gray adds this interesting note:

> 'Scorpions' is explained by Ephraem Syrus as a sadistic elaboration of lashes loaded with leather bags stuffed with sand and armed with spikes; but whether this was a purely Roman invention or an adaptation of local Near Eastern usage and appellation is uncertain.[4]

Verse 15 marks this response as having been in accordance with the Lord's direction. Although both king and people had opportunity to act, the intransigence of Rehoboam was the real weapon that severed the nation.

4. John Gray, *I and II Kings*, p. 306.

ISRAEL'S REBELLION (12:16-20)

With the sounding of the word, "To your tents, O Israel!" (v. 16), the nation was split asunder. A last-ditch attempt to restore order was indicative of the poor advice Rehoboam was receiving. Perhaps to bring about a more conciliatory attitude, he sent Adoram, his chief of forced labor, to work out a peaceful settlement. But this was taken as an act of force by the rebelling tribes. They stoned Rehoboam's ambassador, and the king was forced to flee south to the safety of Jerusalem.

The succinctness of verse 19 points out that, although Rehoboam was responsible for poor administrative judgment, the rebellious tribes were culpable as well. In the Old Testament the Hebrew word *rebellion* is often translated "sin." The aftermath was as Ahijah the prophet had predicted: "None but the tribe of Judah followed the house of David" (v. 20).

REHOBOAM'S THWARTED REPRISAL (12:21-24)

Immediate preparations were made for war. Evidently many Benjamites living on the borders of Judah felt more allegiance to the southern group. Out of the tribes of Judah and Benjamin, Rehoboam was able to muster an army of 180,000 whose mission was to restore the rebellious tribes to a unified kingdom.

This endeavor was checked by the appearance of a prophet, Shemaiah, who said that since Jehovah had ordered the division, any attempt to heal the breach would be contrary to God's will and could only end in disaster for the loyalist army.

### THE BEGINNINGS OF THE ISRAELITE KINGDOM
### 1 Kings 12:25—14:20

Jeroboam was then faced with a splendid opportunity. Had he not received this kingdom by the direct act of Jehovah? Had not Jehovah given him the promise of blessing conditioned upon obedience and recognition of His rule? Had not the God of Israel promised him an enduring house?

Jeroboam threw all these promises away. Instead of becoming a great northern nation, Israel became a nation of great internal strife. The Northern Kingdom would be ruled by nineteen kings in its 253-year existence. Not one king would turn the people back to the worship of Jehovah. Jealousy, strife, and murder would mark the rise and fall of seven dynasties, and contribute to the downfall of two monarchs who did not reign long enough to establish a dynasty. The tragedy was that the seeds that produced this grotesque problem in Israel were planted by Jeroboam, its first king.

## JEROBOAM'S CHANGE IN THE RELIGIOUS AFFAIRS (12:25-33)

Having established his capital at Shechem, Jeroboam began immediate actions to consolidate and secure his new realm. He built Penuel as a border fortress east of the Jordan. This fortress would protect his eastern frontier from Gilead, a territory that had shown unswerving loyalty to the house of David (see 2 Sam 17:27-29). This action met the immediate military problems, but there remained a crisis of far greater consequence—the religious one.

For two generations, pilgrims had journeyed to Jerusalem to participate in the great feasts of the Lord. The Law commanded the males to present themselves before the Lord, especially at the Passover. They were not allowed to kill the paschal lamb in their own towns but were obliged to go to "the place where the LORD your God chooses to establish His name" (Deut 16:6). But, Jeroboam reasoned, "Unless I'm careful, the people will want a descendant of David as their king. When they go to Jerusalem to offer sacrifices at the Temple, they will become friendly with King Rehoboam; then they will kill me and ask him to be their king instead" (1 Kings 12:26-27, TLB).

As Rehoboam had done, Jeroboam turned to counselors. Their advice was essentially, "Do as you wish, Jeroboam. You owe nothing to Rehoboam."

As a result, Jeroboam initiated the religious system which would become the pattern of Israel's sin. Four things characterized this sinful system.

### A new manner of worship (12:28)

In defiance of the first, second, and third commandments of the Law, a representation of God was erected and the announcement given, "Behold your gods, O Israel, that brought you up from the land of Egypt." These were not intended to be rivals for the worship of Jehovah. Wood noted, "As symbols for the new program, he [Jeroboam] erected gold images of calves at each center. The intent was still to worship Yahweh, but in a new way."[5]

### A new place of worship (12:29-31a)

Jeroboam feared that if the people should make pilgrimages to Jerusalem their loyalty would revert to the scion of David. As a preventive measure, Jeroboam set up northern and southern centers of worship at Dan and Bethel. Houses for the golden calves were built in each of the two sacred cities.

### A new priesthood to lead worship (12:31b)

The Aaronic priests and the Levites had fled to the Southern Kingdom as the apostasy of Jeroboam began to be influential. Jeroboam, however, solved this matter easily. He merely designated certain ones as priests, regardless of tribal background.

### A new time for worship (12:32-33)

Although the seventh month was hallowed as the time of the New Year and the Day of Atonement, Jeroboam changed this great festival to the eighth month. His motive was twofold: to break down the mental concept of Jerusalem's importance and to establish a rival system in its place.

5. Leon Wood, *A Survey of Israel's History,* p. 304.

THE PROPHET FROM JUDAH (13:1-32)

*The condemnation of the altar at Bethel (13:1-10)*

A prophet from Judah went to Jeroboam as he was about to burn incense at the altar at Bethel. The prophet uttered a remarkable prophecy. A future son of David, Josiah, would bring retribution upon King Jeroboam for instituting false worship. The prophecy is remarkable because Josiah did not appear in history until 640 B.C., almost eighty years after the Northern Kingdom was gone and almost 300 years after this prophecy was given (see 2 Kings 23:15-20).

As a sign, the altar at Bethel was to be split open and the ashes poured out. Enraged at these words, Jeroboam pointed at the prophet and ordered him to be seized. Jeroboam's hand withered, the altar split open, and the ashes spilled. When the king pleaded for prayer, the prophet entreated the Lord, and the hand was restored.

*The disobedience and death of the prophet (13:11-32)*

The prophet ended his dialogue with Jeroboam by mentioning his directive from the Lord: "You shall eat no bread, nor drink water, nor return by the way which you came" (v. 9). The prophet's exit was short-lived. Tricked by an old prophet, he disregarded the word of God and returned to the old seer's house at Bethel to eat and drink.

The young prophet died for his folly. When he returned southward, he was killed by a lion—a beast obviously prepared by God for this judgment, for the lion did not eat the carcass of the prophet nor disturb his donkey. The old seer brought his body back to Bethel and laid it in his own grave. He then commanded his sons to bury him beside the prophet because his prophecy was genuine. The places of apostasy would be destroyed.

JEROBOAM'S PERSISTENT APOSTASY (13:33—14:20)

Although the king's apostasy was tentatively stopped by his meeting the prophet from Judah, Jeroboam eventually forgot the warning and the sign. He again made priests of any who would volunteer. Their lack of spiritual qualification is evident. This intrusion into prerogatives Jehovah had reserved for Himself would bring about the fall of the house of Jeroboam.

*Ahijah's prophecy against Jeroboam (14:1-18)*

Prompted by the sickness of his son Abijah, Jeroboam sought some word from God. He told his wife to disguise herself and go to Shiloh to Ahijah, who, years before, had foretold Jeroboam's rise to the throne. Ahijah was blind, but had been informed of the ruse. He confronted the king's wife with the deception even as she entered (v. 6). Then he announced to her the extent of God's judgment against Jeroboam for his sin. The king's house would be desolated—no one would remain. In addition, when the queen returned to the capital city and entered her house, her son would die. With this message of horror she returned to Tirzah, and the heir apparent to the throne died.

*The death of Jeroboam (14:19-20)*

After a reign of twenty-two years, Jeroboam died. He was succeeded by a son whose short reign would be terminated violently.

How can one evaluate Jeroboam? There were great moments in his rule; there must be greatness in one who can take the dissident remnants of a rebellion and unite them in a common cause. Yet Jeroboam was insecure, not only because of the threat of his peers, but also because his suspicions led him to doubt God's promises.

## THE SOUTHERN LOYALISTS

### 1 Kings 14:21—15:24

Jeroboam's reign in the North actually bridged the reigns of Rehoboam and Abijam of Judah and extended into the beginning of Asa's rule as well. The reigns of these three Judean kings are briefly traced in this section of Scripture that moves back and forth between the two kingdoms.

A pattern emerges in 1 and 2 Kings. Each ruler is introduced by reference to his age at accession, the number of years he reigned, and any family information. This is followed by a brief account of his accomplishments and sins, significant events during his reign, information concerning his death, and the name of his successor. The material regarding each king in this section is organized under three headings: (1) the introductory background, (2) the significance of the reign, and (3) the summary of his reign and death.

### THE REIGN OF REHOBOAM (14:21-31; cf. 2 CHRON 10:1—12:16)

*The introductory background (14:21)*

Having begun his reign at the age of forty-one, Rehoboam ruled for seventeen years. The kings of Judah all reigned in Jerusalem, a note that is a fitting reference to God's faithfulness. The mention of the Ammonite background of Rehoboam's mother is especially interesting in its religious implications.

*The significance of the reign (14:22-28)*

The information in 1 Kings is sketchy at this point, but 2 Chronicles supplements the account.

Two important events occurred in Rehoboam's reign. The first was the developing apostasy and immorality of his subjects. To this point, none had offended the holiness of God to the extent of Judah's offense. The people returned to the practices of the

Canaanites before them. These included not only idolatry, but also the most gross sexual practices.

The second important event in the reign of Rehoboam was the invasion of Judah by Shishak. This Egyptian monarch is also known as Sheshonk I, founder of the twenty-second dynasty. The invasion was well recorded. An account of it appears on the wall of the temple at Karnak, Egypt. The parallel record in 2 Chronicles 12:2-9 adds information to the short Kings narrative. The invasion not only affected Judah, but, according to Sheshonk's account, brought his authority as far as the strategic city of Megiddo.

Sheshonk's invasion was costly to Judah. The vast treasury of gold that had been accumulated by Solomon was all but decimated at the hands of the Egyptians. The 200 shields of beaten gold were replaced with shields of cheaper bronze. The polished bronze undoubtedly gave an excellent and beautiful glow, but it had not the natural, unpolished beauty of gold. One wonders how many times God's people have tried to substitute brass for refined gold in their service to the Lord. One other noteworthy fact is that the shields no longer hung in the great chamber. They were instead kept in the guards' room, and runners carried them before the king in great pomp when he entered the house of the Lord.

### The summary of his reign and death (14:29-31)

Continual turbulence marked the first seventeen years of the divided kingdom. Although no detailed account is given, the animosity engendered by the two factions probably caused many border skirmishes not unlike those that occur these days in the same part of the world. The death of Rehoboam is tersely recorded, and his successor named.

THE REIGN OF ABIJAM (15:1-8; cf. 2 CHRON 13:1—14:1)

### The introductory background (15:1-2)

Little is known of Abijam, Solomon's grandson. His accession to the throne occurred near the end of Jeroboam's reign in Israel. For three years Abijam was the guardian of the slipping kingdom of Judah. If one assumes that he was thirty-seven at accession, it is interesting that his death occurred when he was at the height of manhood. His mother, Maacah, was probably the granddaughter of David's son Absalom. Keil agrees with this position, noting the genealogical line.[6]

## *The significance of the reign (15:3-6)*

Much of what is recorded here about Abijam is recorded because God honored His promise to David. However, Abijam's sin was well marked. Following in the steps of his father, Abijam continued those sins. The passage indicates that his reign was not one of outright apostasy, but rather one of creeping compromise. Second Chronicles 13 notes that Abijam's military forces won a decisive victory over those of Jeroboam because Judah called upon the Lord (2 Chron 13:4-20). This defeat was a direct cause of Jeroboam's subsequent loss of strength, and death.

## *The summary of his reign and death (15:7-8)*

The wars between Abijam and Jeroboam are summarized in one statement. Abijam's death opened the way for the accession of Asa.

### THE REIGN OF ASA (15:9-14; cf. 2 CHRON 14:2—16:14)

Five of Judah's kings stood in marked contrast to the others. Asa was one of these whose reigns were characterized by godliness. As a result of his influence, Asa's son came to be known as one of the good kings. Example is important, but at times exemplary conduct fails to bring about settled conditions. Following a period of over a half century of good rule, deterioration set in.

6. C. F. Keil and Franz Delitzsch, *Biblical Commentary on the Old Testament*, vol. 6, *The Books of the Kings*, by C. F. Keil, p. 217.

*The introductory background (15:9-10)*

Acceding to the throne near the end of his northern rival's reign, Asa was to reign for a period of forty-one years. The biographical entry concerning his mother appears to indicate that Asa's father, Abijam, had married his own mother. A more acceptable explanation is offered by Keil:

> "The name of his mother was Maacah, the daughter of Absalom." This notice, which agrees verbatim with verse 2, cannot mean that Abijam had his own mother for a wife; though Thenius finds this meaning in the passage, and then proceeds to build up conjectures concerning emendations of the text. We must rather explain it . . . as signifying that Maacah, the mother of Abijam, continued during Asa's reign to retain the post of queen-mother . . . till Asa deposed her on account of her idolatry (verse 13), probably because Asa's own mother had died at an early age.[7]

*The significance of his reign (15:11-22)*

Asa was characterized by doing "what was right in the sight of the Lord." The most important event of his reign was the great religious reform—a reform somewhat nurtured by the prophecy and encouragement of the prophet Azariah (2 Chron 15). Idolatry and its practices had been allowed from the latter part of Solomon's reign through the rule of the first two monarchs of the divided kingdom. It was time for a thorough purge. The mention of Asa's reforms reveals the extent of the depravity that had become common. Canaanite religion included both male and female prostitutes. These were put away, and the idols destroyed. The queen mother, Maacah, was also removed, and her worship of the Canaanite fertility-goddess, Asherah, was ended.

Verse 14 presents one of the ominous notes that appear so frequently regarding reforms: "But the high places were not taken away." The account in Chronicles states that Asa "removed the

7. Ibid., p. 218.

foreign altars and high places" (2 Chron 14:3). Probably the solution to this seeming discrepancy is that since such altars on the high places included those dedicated to Jehovah worship, the idolatrous ones were destroyed, but the ones dedicated to Israel's God were illegally allowed to remain.

Reform always centered on a return to a true worship connected with the Temple. Verse 15 refers to the restored centrality of this sacred place during Asa's reign.

This good king's rule was marked not only by religious reform, but by military successes and prudent alliances. The military achievements included the annexation of Ramah as a military border guard for Judah. In an effort to keep Israel and Judah separate, Baasha of Israel had made Ramah his central fortress. Asa decided to bring upon Baasha pressure from the north which would weaken his position in the south. This pressure could best be applied by the Aramaean king, Ben-hadad I.* The alliance was successful. Baasha withdrew from Ramah, and Asa's forces moved in to dismantle the fortress. With the confiscated building materials, Asa built border strongholds to the north and east of Ramah (Mizpah and Ramah).

Chronicles recounts yet another military campaign—that against Zerah the Ethiopian (2 Chron 14:9-15). The significant feature of this campaign was the way in which Asa countered. Asa's army numbered 580,000 (2 Chron 14:8). His foe came with 1,000,000 troops and 300 chariots—hardly the conditions for a Judahite victory. But in this situation, Asa did not make any foreign alliances. He prayed, and Jehovah routed the Ethiopians. They fled southward before the rapidly advancing forces of Judah. The Egyptian invasion resulted in material prosperity

*I have labeled Ben-hadad I as king of Aram rather than Syria. *Aram* is found in the Hebrew. *Syria* was adopted from the Septuagint text, and, though the name Syria gives a locale, it does not identify the origin of the people living there at the time of these events. The people were not Syrians; they were a Semitic people from southern Mesopotamia who had traveled northward, finally settling in the area north of Palestine. Their capital was Damascus.

for Judah through the vast amount of booty taken (2 Chron 14:14-15).

### *The summary of his reign and death (15:23-24)*

Asa is remembered because of the administrative strengths he evidenced in his military victories and building achievements. Others have noted that the Kings' account contains what is not a normal entry—Asa's feet were diseased. Two reasons have been adduced for his problems: First, he responded in an ungodly manner to the rebuke by the prophet Hanani, and second, he failed to consult Jehovah concerning the disease (2 Chron 16: 7-10, 12). But his reign of forty-one years added stability to the Southern Kingdom. That stability would continue through the reign of his son.

## REVOLUTION IN ISRAEL

### 1 Kings 15:25—16:21

#### THE FALL OF THE HOUSE OF JEROBOAM (15:25-31)

The account now returns to the history of Israel. The heir apparent to Israel's throne, Abijah, had died. His brother Nadab acceded to the throne. Historically, the record reverts almost thirty-nine years to early in Asa's reign. Nadab's two-year reign, based on non-accession year dating, was probably a reign of one year or less. Little is noted of him except that he continued in the sin of Jeroboam.

Conspiracy erupted into action as Baasha and his followers murdered Jeroboam on the battlefield at Gibbethon in Philistia. In an effort to insure his position, Baasha annihilated all the members of Jeroboam's household. Thus, Jehovah punished the sin of unbelief exhibited in Jeroboam and continued in the reign of his son. The first dynasty of Israel ended violently.

## THE SHORT-LIVED DYNASTY OF BAASHA (15:32—16:14)

Baasha's history has already been partially traced. A terse statement regarding his wars with Asa begins the short narrative of his reign. Baasha was followed by his son, Elah, who extended the dynastic power of Baasha by about a year.

### The reign of Baasha (15:32—16:7)

Characterized by evil, the most notable thing about Baasha's reign was the prophetic warning delivered by Jehu the son of Hanani (16:2-4). Having briefly recounted the king's sins, Jehu announced the judgment of God upon his house. The record then accounts for his death and burial at Tirzah. Seemingly, a reign of twenty-four years should be recognized by more than this short account. But the scriptural principle seems to be that a life lived out of fellowship with God is of little importance.

### The reign of Elah and the fall of the dynasty (16:8-14)

Elah continued his father's policies and paid no heed to the warning of Hanani. As Nadab before him, Elah too became the victim of a conspiracy. Gray suggests that Zimri was a specialist in chariot warfare.[8] As such, he would have commanded a very powerful element in the army. Attacking Elah while the king was debauching himself into a drunken stupor, Zimri continued the revolution by removing any possibility of revenge as he wiped out Baasha's entire household.

## THE SHORTEST REIGN IN ISRAEL'S HISTORY (16:15-20)

Zimri, ascending the throne in much the same way Baasha had, would have been expected to insure stability. The geographical locations give some clue why this was not so. The Israelite army was again at Gibbethon of Philistia. The assassination of Elah took place at Tirzah, the capital, which was a

8. Gray, p. 361.

four- or five-day march for an army or a two-day journey for a runner. This accounts for the seven days. The encamped military forces under Omri left the siege of Gibbethon to return to the capital. Tirzah was no enemy city to the returning troops and probably offered but token resistance. Realizing the folly of his unilateral action, Zimri retired to the palace and committed suicide by setting it on fire.

## A DIVIDED HOUSE (16:21-28)

The fortunes of Israel had augured great power and influence during Jeroboam's reign. But the declension that marked the succeeding rulers resulted, with the death of Zimri, in two opposing factions.

### Tibni, the son of Ginath

Tibni was one of those characters in the biblical drama who made a sudden appearance and as sudden an exit. Yet by comparing 1 Kings 16:15 and 16:23, one discovers that this man was a formidable force in Israel for about three years. The fact that there was a division in the Northern Kingdom at this time is especially interesting in light of the divided nation later when Pekah and Menahem reigned concurrently. Perhaps the seeds of division were sown in the ninth century B.C. and reaped in the eighth.

### Omri, the commander of the army

The second faction—the triumphant one—was led by Omri. Since the Israelite army was his chief claim to power, it is even more surprising that Omri's accession to the throne took three years. Finally, however, the unrest and uncertainty of leadership was brought to an end with his victorious rise to the throne. His dynasty marked the low point in the religious apostasy of Israel as is seen in the succeeding chapter.

## SUMMARY

Extending from 931-30 B.C., a period of almost six decades, Israel to the north had experienced two coups, three dynastic changes, and a three-year civil war. Those sixty years could hardly be viewed as a period of consolidation. The civil war won by Omri was an event that did bring political strength to the Northern Kingdom, but one through which her religious apostasy sank to new levels.

In the south, the house of David was all but emasculated by the defection of the ten northern tribes. However, through the reigns of Rehoboam and Abijam, the Southern Kingdom's power and influence were gradually strengthened. In spite of great losses to Sheshonk I, Judah was the recipient of God's intervention when, against overwhelming odds, she was victorious over Zerah of Ethiopia. As Asa's long reign continued, the national fortunes of Judah looked increasingly optimistic. The worship of Jehovah was dominant, and this situation remained stable through the reign of Asa's son, Jehoshaphat.

The religious apostasy of Jeroboam gives further evidence of the results of unbelief. As the nation had forgotten God's promises in the wilderness of Paran (Num 12:16—14:10), so Jeroboam was unwilling to be committed to God's promise of success and perpetuity. He led the Northern Kingdom in religious defection.

# 4

## Elijah and the Reign of Ahab

### 1 Kings 16:29—22:40

The most infamous king of the notorious Omride dynasty had reigned during Elijah's ministry. Perhaps it would be more accurate to say that God raised up Elijah for such a time as the days of Ahab.

Ahab came to the throne in 874 B.C., and his twenty-two-year reign ended in 853 B.C. His notoriety is clearly stated: Ahab "did evil in the sight of the LORD more than all who were before him" (v. 30). Expanding on this statement, the writer refers to Ahab's marriage to the Sidonian princess, Jezebel, and the subsequent establishment of Baalism as the religion of the north. Almost anticipating the extent of Ahab's disobedience and resulting judgment, the chronicler adds a note concerning an attempt to rebuild Jericho by Hiel the Bethelite, and the cost of that disobedience (16:34). In such a time, God raised up the prophet Elijah.

### THE BEGINNING MINISTRY OF THE PROPHET ELIJAH

### 1 Kings 17:1—19:21

Elijah's prophetic ministry dominates this section of the book. Three distinct accounts of the prophet's activity are interspersed with an account of Ahab's rule. The first section concerning Elijah is the most lengthy (1 Kings 17:1—19:21). These three chapters contain four separate though continuous accounts: (1)

the prediction of the drought, (2) the events of Zarephath, (3) the contest on the mountains of Carmel and the ensuing rain, and (4) Elijah's flight to Mount Horeb at the threat of Jezebel.

### THE PREDICTION OF DROUGHT (17:1-7)

Appearing suddenly on the scene, Elijah stood before Ahab and announced a three-and-one-half-year drought. It was probably unnecessary for Elijah to give a reason for the drought since Ahab would have had some awareness of sin. Seldom is a recipient of God's discipline ignorant of the reason. Following the announcement, the Lord directed Elijah to travel to what was probably one of the last available water supplies. There he was to hide. Why hide? Obviously the drought would be blamed on him, and indeed it was. This is evident from the events that transpired when Obadiah met the prophet.

The brook Cherith is said to have been "east of the Jordan" (v. 3). Elijah, being an "east-Jordanian" from Gilead, probably knew the area well. There the Lord sustained him with water and with bread and meat brought by ravens. However, soon the water was gone, and Elijah received new direction.

### THE EVENTS OF ZAREPHATH (17:8-24)

God's directions are not always easy to understand. His next directive sent Elijah into Jezebel's home territory. He went to Zarephath where God had already "commanded a widow" to care for him. When Elijah met the woman at the city gates, it was evident that the drought had spread over the borders of Israel into Phoenicia as well. The prophet asked for something to eat and drink. By her reply he would know if she were the one whom God had prepared. Her answer made evident her poverty. Elijah told her she would have ample flour and oil for the duration of the drought. Luke records an interesting commentary by the Lord concerning this (Luke 4:25-26). Elijah did not go to Zarephath to hide. He rather went as a prophet to edify, exhort, and console this outcast.*

A more serious problem arose in the household: the widow's son died. That he was really dead is accepted by most expositors. At this point, it is interesting to observe the reaction of the widow. She believed that this tragedy was brought upon her because of some past sin. Keil was correct in commenting that her response was born out of the heathen background in which she lived, though there was "at the same time a mind susceptible to divine truth and conscious of its sin, to which the Lord could not refuse His aid."[1]

Elijah took the child and *prayed*. His prayer was not one of request. It was one of perplexity. He was uncertain as to God's purpose in the death of the child. This prayer reminds one that James uses Elijah's praying as an example, noting that he was "a man with a nature like ours" (James 5:17). That nature is quite evident here; God's prophet experienced perplexity. He did not, however, remain in its mire; he took action that brought a new turn to prayer. He then prayed, "O LORD my God, I pray Thee, let this child's life return to him" (1 Kings 17:21). The Lord answered by returning the child to life.

## THE CONTEST OF THE MOUNTAINS OF CARMEL (18:1-46)

### The meeting with Obadiah (18:1-19)

The drought was about to be broken. For three and one-half years the Lord had sustained the prophet, and for the same period Ahab had heard nothing from Elijah. But the drought and the accompanying famine were grim reminders of the prophet's words.

Obadiah was the king's chief steward. He was also a worshiper of Jehovah, and, obviously unknown to Ahab, he had hidden

---

*For the work of a prophet, cf. 1 Cor 14:3.

1. C. F. Keil and Franz Delitzsch, *Biblical Commentary on the Old Testament*, vol. 6, *The Books of the Kings*, by C. F. Keil, p. 239.

100 prophets of the Lord. Sent by Ahab to look for water, Obadiah was confronted by Elijah. Such a meeting, if seen by the wrong people, would have meant death for Obadiah (v. 9), and he was afraid to tell Ahab that Elijah wished an audience. Obadiah remarked on Elijah's tendencies to appear and disappear, and he was afraid he might be left "holding the bag." But Elijah prevailed. Obadiah talked to the king who then came out to meet Elijah.

Greeted by Ahab with "Is this you, you troubler of Israel?" (v. 17), Elijah quickly countered with the truth: Ahab was the real troubler of Israel. The judgment of God was Ahab's reward for idolatry. Concisely, Elijah then challenged Ahab to gather the prophets of Baal and Asherah at Mount Carmel.

## The challenge of Jehovah to Baal (18:20-36)

When the people gathered, Elijah asked them, "How long will you hesitate between two opinions?" (v. 21). The word "hesitate" signifies a limping motion. Elijah's words indicated that the people had not repudiated the worship of Jehovah, but had accommodated it to the sensual worship of Baal and Asherah. The people remained silent, and Elijah issued his challenge to the 450 prophets of Baal. The implication was that since Baal was considered the god of heavens, he should be able to demonstrate his power from the heavens. A sacrifice would be prepared, and the fire for the sacrifice was to come down from heaven. If Baal were God, then Baal would send fire to consume the sacrifice. If Jehovah were God, He would demonstrate His power in the same way.

And so the rivalry began. Elijah offered the priests of Baal the first opportunity. After all, if they were successful, there would be no further contest. But success evaded them. For almost six hours Elijah remained silent as through the morning hours the priests called upon Baal. At noon Elijah could stand the silence no longer, and he taunted, "Call louder . . . Perhaps he has gone aside (v. 27, author's paraphrase). The Hebrew at this point is more direct than most English translations. Some commentators and translators have suggested that Elijah's biting irony insinuated that Baal was indisposed because he was taking care of his physical functions.*

Elijah's jabs further frustrated the prophets, and they called louder. The sun began its descent in the western sky. Still "there was no voice, no one answered, and no one paid attention" (v. 29).

Then, in marked contrast, Elijah called the people near. Building an altar, he used twelve stones to call to their attention the association and relationships that were theirs. After he had prepared the altar so as to prevent any claim of trickery, Elijah readied the sacrifice. He then calmly called upon Jehovah to answer. The silence was shattered as fire fell from heaven.

Pandemonium broke out. The people fell on their faces and acknowledged Jehovah. But the contest was not ended. In the gathering darkness, the people pursued the fleeing prophets down the mountain to the Kishon River and there slaughtered them.

### *The breaking of the drought (18:41-46)*

Ahab had been told that rain would come. Now Elijah dispatched his servant to the mountaintop to watch the western sky. Soon a small cloud appeared, and Elijah directed Ahab to leave before flooding would make travel impossible. Soon after Ahab left, the sky was black with clouds, and the rains began to fall. In spite of his chariot and his early lead, Ahab found Elijah at Jezreel waiting for him (v. 46).

### ELIJAH'S FLIGHT TO MOUNT HOREB AT THE THREAT OF JEZEBEL (19:1-21)

Three natural divisions occur in this section. The shortest of these deals with the threat by Jezebel (19:1-2). The longer

*Gray, *I and II Kings,* pp. 397-98.

sections recount Elijah's journey to Horeb (19:3-8) and Jehovah's revelation and commission to Elijah (19:9-21). The chapter is a practical one because it furnishes a reminder to God's people that depression can follow a great venture in God's work. Elijah failed to observe this principle operating in his own situation, and thus he failed to prepare himself either mentally or spiritually for it.

### Jezebel's threat (19:1-2)

Ahab recounted to his wife the day's events and the resultant slaughter of the prophets of Baal. Whether or not Ahab had thoughts of revenge is unstated. But Jezebel undoubtedly saw that all her labor to institute Baal worship was about to be lost, and this she would not passively accept. Attacking the problem at what she believed to be the core, she sent a threatening message to Elijah. Invoking an oath, she threatened to do to Elijah what he had ordered done to her prophets. As with many such oaths, this one failed to bring about either the death of the seer or her own.

### Elijah's journey to Horeb (19:3-8)

Fearful for his life, the prophet ran. In one terse statement, the chronicler brings him to Beersheba, over seventy miles away. This was not his destination. It was merely the last prominent settlement on the edge of the Negeb. Leaving his servant there, Elijah went a day's journey and rested under a juniper (broom) tree.

And there God met his needs. Elijah—faithless, discouraged, no doubt tired from his journey, and certainly not obeying God's directives to him as a prophet—was fed by God. One thinks God should have reprimanded him. But that could wait. The prophet had a journey to make, and God prepared him physically for it. It was quite a meal, for in its strength Elijah continued traveling southward for forty days, until he reached the mountain of God, Horeb (also Sinai).

He entered a cave and there was confronted by the Lord. The Lord's question "What are you doing here?" was a rebuke to the prophet. He had not been called to be a guru on a mountain. God's prophet was to be engaged in the mainstream of life. But Elijah was choosing to withdraw. His reply was that, in spite of his zeal for Jehovah, his efforts had met only scorn and rebellion, and had resulted in death for the Lord's prophets. "I alone am left; and they seek my life," Elijah complained.

Then Jehovah passed by, and three startling demonstrations occurred: a fantastic wind that broke rocks into pieces, an earthquake, and then a fire. But Jehovah was in none of them. These were followed by the "sound of a gentle blowing."

> Tempest, earthquake, and fire, which are even more terrible in the awful solitude of the Horeb mountains than in an inhabited land, are signs of the coming of the Lord's judgment. . . . It was in the midst of such terrible phenomena that the Lord had once come down upon Sinai, to inspire the people who were assembled at the foot of the mountain with a salutary dread of His terrible majesty, of the fiery zeal of His wrath and love, which consumes whatever opposes it. . . . But now the Lord was not in these terrible phenomena; to signify to the prophet that He did not work in His earthly kingdom with the destroying zeal of the wrath, or with the pitiless severity of judgment. It was in a soft, gentle rustling that He revealed Himself to him.[2]

Elijah responded by standing at the cave entrance. Again he was asked, "What are you doing here, Elijah?" He repeated his complaint, but there was no reprimand. Instead came a renewed commission. Three responsibilities were given the prophet. First, he was to go to Damascus to anoint Hazael king over Syria; sec-

2. Keil, p. 258.

ond, he was to anoint Jehu king over Israel; and third, he was to anoint Elisha as prophet in his place.

Only the last duty was carried out immediately. The other two occurred during Elisha's ministry. Why then do they appear here? Some have suggested that Elijah did go to Damascus, but that his visit was not recorded. The text, however, seems to indicate that he went to Elisha first. If so, Elisha's commission was that he continue Elijah's ministry.

Encouraged by the knowledge that seven thousand in Israel still followed Jehovah, Elijah made his way down the treacherous cliffs of Sinai, traveled back across the wilderness of the Negeb, and met Elisha. Elijah cast his mantle on him, and Elisha recognized the great call he was receiving. Following a sacrificial meal, the two left.

## THE ISRAELITE-SYRIAN WARS

### 1 Kings 20:1—22:53

The emphasis on Elijah is discontinued temporarily, and the text returns to an account of Ahab's reign. This section treats Ahab more favorably than preceding chapters. Some therefore have concluded that this passage is evidence of a new source of material. The account describes three campaigns of Israel against the Syrians. The Syrian king Ben-hadad should probably be identified as Ben-hadad II. Three Syrian kings who bore this name appear in the historical books. The first is to be linked with the rule of Asa in Judah. The third appears in 2 Kings 13 during the reigns of Jehoahaz and Hazael.

The Syrian ruler mentioned in this section was greedy for land. Though Ahab was an able administrator and had strengthened the defenses of the capital city Samaria, he had not prepared an army to meet the threat of the emerging powers around him.

### THE FIRST CAMPAIGN (20:1-25)

Ben-hadad laid siege to the capital and attempted to intimidate

Ahab into an easy surrender. It seems that at first Ahab capitulated, but Ben-hadad sensed that he could gain more and pressed harder (vv. 5-6). This led to a counsel of war. The elders counseled the king not to listen to Ben-hadad's demands. Ahab returned a message to the Syrian that he would not comply. Ben-hadad invoked a curse on Ahab that was similar to the curse Jezebel had invoked on Elijah. He boasted that Israel would be ground to dust. Ahab's reply was, paraphrased: "Don't count your chickens before they hatch" (see v. 11). And the siege began.

"But God"—how often those words are implied or stated in Scripture. A prophet of the Lord came to Ahab with encouragement. Jehovah promised victory, and the initiator of the battle was to be the underdog Israelites. Seven thousand Israelites went out in the heat of the day and routed the northern invaders (vv. 16-21). The Syrians fled back across their borders and, in debriefings, came to the conclusion that they had lost because Jehovah was the god of the mountains. If the geographical location for battle could be changed, they decided Israel would be defeated. With that confidence they regrouped.

But the Israelites were not idle. Recognizing the divine intervention, they were obedient to prepare for a renewed effort by the Syrians a year later.

THE SECOND CAMPAIGN (20:26-43)

The next time the Syrians assembled at Aphek, which was located in the rolling plains country of the Trans-Jordan. To the Syrians, the geography was at least favorable. The pitiful situation of the Israelites is tersely stated in verse 27: "The sons of Israel camped before them like two little flocks of goats, but the Syrians filled the country." Again, divine assurance came through a prophet of God. The battle was short but decisive. The total casualties were 127,000 Syrians. The battle, however, would be costly for Israel's king. Because Ahab spared Ben-hadad's life, a future battle would result in Ahab's death and the defeat of his forces.

The land of Israel relaxed after the victory, and during the period of peace, Ahab turned to internal matters. Coveting property adjacent to the palace in Jezreel, Ahab met with its owner Naboth and attempted to trade for it or buy it. Naboth refused because of the inheritance rights that protected his land. His refusal depressed Ahab, who seemingly was subject to fits of dejection during this time (see 20:43; 21:4-5). Discussing with Jezebel his desire for the vineyard triggered in her a crafty plot to kill Naboth and thus allow Ahab to take the property. Directed by Jezebel, the men of Naboth's city accused him of blasphemy, and took him outside the city, and stoned him.

This led to a reappearance of Elijah (vv. 17-24) who confronted the king. Elijah declared Jehovah's word to him: Ahab's days were numbered. His dynasty was coming to a speedy end. Even the death of the queen would become a by-word: "The dogs shall eat Jezebel in the district of Jezreel."

The editor's comment in 21:25-26 noted the extent of the idolatry promoted by Ahab and his queen. To the chronicler, Ahab's religion was a reinstitution of the system that had been so harshly condemned by the Lord. The prophet's words had a positive effect on the king. He evidently acknowledged Jehovah and confessed his sin before Him. For that reason, the Lord delayed the execution of judgment until after Ahab's death.

THE THIRD CAMPAIGN (22:1-40)

First Kings concludes with the account of the third crucial campaign and its aftermath. Historically a very important battle, it occurred in the last year of Ahab's reign, 853 B.C. Ahab and Ben-hadad II allied against the rising power of Assyria led by Shalmaneser II, and met the Assyrians at the Orontes River at Qarqar. The battle did have a delaying effect on the Assyrian conquests and probably led in some way to a renewal of hostility between Israel and Syria.

In the same year, Ahab decided to regain Israel's lost area of Ramoth-Gilead east of the Jordan. On friendly terms with Judah at that time, Ahab enlisted the assistance of Judah's King Jehoshaphat who, being a worshiper of Jehovah, agreed upon the condition that an inquiry be made of the Lord (v. 5). Ahab gathered some four hundred prophets and faced them with the question of his anticipated action against Ramoth-Gilead. Ahab's seers all agreed that he should go up and that the Lord would give him success. Jehoshaphat was not convinced. There may be a hint of sarcasm in his question: "Is there not yet a prophet of the Lord here, that we may inquire of him?" Ahab reluctantly told him that there was a prophet named Micaiah, but Ahab did not like Micaiah because he prophesied evil against the king. When Jehoshaphat insisted, Micaiah was summoned. As the kings waited for him to appear, the other prophets continued to encourage Ahab (vv. 11-12).

Micaiah was instructed not to deviate from the words already spoken. In a moment of irony, he did speak of military success, but then predicted the death of Ahab and the scattering of Israel's army (vv. 17-23). Micaiah was imprisoned for such treasonable words, and Ahab and Jehoshaphat went off to battle. Ahab took precautions by disguising himself, but this did not prevent God's judgment. "A certain man drew his bow at random" (v. 34), and the king of Israel was struck down. Elijah's prophecy was fulfilled, for dogs licked up the royal blood as soldiers washed the king's chariot in the pool the prostitutes used for bathing.

Ahab's reign was marked by gross disobedience. But the chronicler did note his building enterprises and his "ivory house." Archaeologists have found many remnants of wood inlaid with ivory. Many of these are on display in the Hebrew Museum in Jerusalem.

## SUMMARY

Elijah's work was almost concluded. He was evidently an old man when he fled for his life. His voice illustrates the truth that God always has a witness. He also has a remnant. Elijah had viewed himself as a lone warrior against all of the hosts of Baal, but he was not alone after all. It should be noted that the Lord's work is not thwarted because of the disobedience of a servant. New servants are appointed, and God's purposes continue to be fulfilled.

# 5

## Elisha, the Man of the Spirit

### 1 Kings 22:40–2 Kings 9:13

The ministries of Elijah and Elisha dominate the closing chapters of 1 Kings and the opening chapters of 2 Kings. The chronicler's normal formula is merely incidental to a portrayal of the careers of these two prophets.

With the death of Ahab, Elijah's work was almost completed. That which follows is both epilogue and prologue. It is an epilogue to the amazing ministry of the Tishbite, but a prologue to the account of him who asked and received a double portion of Elijah's spiritual power.

### THE HISTORICAL SETTING

### 1 Kings 22:41—2 Kings 1:18

The historian here resumes his method of keeping records. With the death of the northern monarch, Ahab, he turns to a review of the background of the southern king, Jehoshaphat. The Judean king has already appeared in the record, but his background has not been explained. Chapter 22 records the alliance between the two Jewish states and their conflict against Syria, and there Jehoshaphat is named (vv. 2, 4, 5, 7, etc.). In the last section of 1 Kings, his career is summarized.

#### THE REIGN OF JEHOSHAPHAT (1 Kings 22:41-50)

The account of Jehoshaphat's twenty-five years of rule is condensed into ten verses. The parallel account is in 2 Chronicles

20. The dates of his reign are marked from Ahab's fourth year. It should be remembered that Ahab reigned for twenty-two years, and it is noted in 1 Kings 22:51 that Ahaziah, Ahab's son, came to the throne in Jehoshaphat's seventeenth year. The slight discrepancy here can be resolved on the basis of accession- versus nonaccession-year dating.

Jehoshaphat is remembered as one of the good kings of Judah of whom there had been thus far but one other, Asa. He is remembered for carrying on the reforms instituted by his father. The nagging problem of false worship centers on the high places continued, however, but the perversion of homosexuality was sternly handled by the Judean monarch.

The Southern Kingdom had considerable political influence as well. The note of 1 Kings 22:47 that "there was no king in Edom" refers to the subjugation of the Edomites to Judah during this time. This achievement allowed open passage to the Red Sea, and led Jehoshaphat to undertake an ambitious plan for a merchant marine venture—one which ended in disaster precipitated either by a storm or very poor navigation. Some commentators believe that it was the latter. Whatever the reason, the northern king offered to aid Jehoshaphat by lending him some of his more experienced Israelite sailors. In spite of military alliances with the Israelite kings, Jehoshaphat refused to enter into a joint commercial enterprise. With the death of Jehoshaphat, a long period of spiritual growth came to an end. Jehoram, his successor, would accomplish nothing of value during his days.

THE REIGN OF AHAZIAH (1 Kings 22:52—2 Kings 1:18)

The short, less than two-year, reign of Ahab's successor, Ahaziah, is important because it demonstrates the results of emphasizing idolatrous practices. Also during this reign the last recorded prophetic act of the venerable Elijah was performed. Ahaziah's rule was marked by more of the same policies instituted under his idolatrous mother and promulgated by his weak-willed father.

Very soon after his accession Ahaziah was faced with rebellion. Moab, which had served as a vassal kingdom to Israel for many years, was led in a rebellion prompted no doubt by Ahab's sudden death on the battlefield and Israel's concurrent defeat. Faced with insurrection, and possibly in a moment of shock, the young king lost his balance and was severely injured in a fall.

Having been thoroughly immersed in the worship of Baal, he considered but one course of action. He dispatched his servants to the Philistine city Ekron to consult with the priests of Baal-zebub (lord of the flies). Baal-zebub was believed to be a god of healing powers.

Elijah was commanded to intercept the contingent from the palace. He remonstrated with them about their effrontery in consulting pagan gods and directed them to tell the king he would soon die. Deterred from their mission by the impressive figure of the prophet, they returned to the king and gave him the message.

The servants' descriptions of the messenger quickly identified him as Elijah. Ahaziah decided to capture the prophet, but Elijah, acting under Jehovah's protection, was preserved from two groups of fifty each. The captain of a third group begged for mercy, and the prophet, instructed by the angel of the Lord, spared him and his soldiers. Elijah then accompanied them to the king's bedside where he repeated the ominous message that the king's servants had delivered earlier.

As God had ordained, Ahaziah died. Ahaziah was evidently quite young and was not succeeded by a son. Instead, a younger brother, Jehoram, succeeded him to the throne. During Jehoram's reign, kings in both the north and the south bore the same name.

## Elisha's Ministry to Israel
### 2 Kings 2:1—9:13

The times in which Elisha ministered to Israel were times of great crises. Defeat at the hands of the Syrians, loss of political prestige demonstrated in the rebellion of Moab, and moral decay brought on by the idolatrous worship of Baal all contributed to a climate of uneasiness, poverty, and international concern. But Elisha was a man equal to his task. He is immediately viewed as one who understood the nature of his call, but who also recognized the power needed to accomplish its responsibilities.

## THE TRANSLATION OF ELIJAH (2:1-14)

Important to the transfer of divine power was the bargain made by Elisha with the departing prophet. Elijah agreed that his successor could receive a double portion of his spirit on the condition that he be a participant in the aged prophet's departure. This was not a light agreement. Receiving a double portion was the inheritance advantage of the firstborn. Elijah considered the bestowal of a double portion of his spirit as a sign from God.

Three times Elijah asked Elisha not to follow him, but Elisha would have none of that. Each time Elijah mentioned a location to which he was going, Elisha stayed with him. To Bethel, to Jericho, and then to the Jordan they traveled together. They were not alone, for fifty of their students accompanied them almost as far as the Jordan. These stood at a distance while the two prophets approached the river. As Elijah and Elisha descended the bank to the water's edge, Elijah took his mantle, folded it together, and struck the waters. Then, as the children of Israel had done almost six hundred years earlier, these two walked to the eastern shore on dry ground.

There Elisha received the commitment of the double portion of Elijah's spirit. There the condition was fulfilled, for Elisha witnessed a fantastic event. Appearing suddenly between the two prophets was a chariot of fire drawn by fiery horses, and they took Elijah into heaven. As he departed, the mantle of power and authority fell away. Elisha was left on his own. Returning to the river bank, he asked, "Where is the LORD, the God of Elijah?" As Elijah had done before him, he struck the waters with the mantle, and Elijah's God demonstrated that He was Elisha's God as well. The prophet crossed to the western bank on dry ground.

### THE DEMONSTRATION OF HIS CALL (2:15-25)

Folowing his return across the Jordan, Elisha was faced with three situations that authenticated his call as Elijah's successor.

#### *His authority (2:15-18)*

The young disciples who had waited near the west bank of the Jordan recognized the change of leadership. This was probably evidenced by Elisha's possession of the mantle. They showed respect and submission by bowing down before him. Then they desired that fifty athletic men search the ravines and mountains for Elijah in case the whirlwind that took him away had put him down again. At first Elisha forbade their search. However, he changed his order at their insistence. But three days of combing the ravines and hills were unfruitful, and the young men returned. Elisha reminded them of the counsel he had given in the beginning. Doubtless, to these young students, the experience marked Elisha as a man of leadership.

#### *His power (2:19-22)*

Elisha's *power* is distinguished from his *authority* in the sense of demonstrating the miraculous. The citizens of Jericho were faced with a problem. This ancient city of palms (Deut 34:3) had trouble with its water supply. Located in one of the few fertile areas in the desolate wilderness near the Jordan, the site of Jericho had been inhabited for hundreds of years. The phrase of verse 19, "the land is unfruitful," literally means, "the land causes barrenness." The average reader would assume this means the water had mineral deposits that prevented growth. But the problem may also have been related to human life. John Gray reports that a recent study of the region shows that certain springs in the area have contacted radioactive strata. The combining of these substances with the water has polluted the water in such a way to cause sterility.[1] This could easily explain the problem at Jericho. The unstable strata of the region could have shifted so as to bring radioactive deposits into the channel of the spring.

But the cure was hardly the result of the shifting strata. It was clearly miraculous. Elisha ordered a new jar, filled it with salt, and poured the contents into the spring. There was instant success. When the historian noted that the waters were purified "to this day," he could have added more than two millennia to that figure. The spring is still the principle source of water for that region, and its flow provides much more water today than was needed in Elisha's day.

## His acknowledgment (2:23-24)

Leaders have always had to deal with disrespect. In Western society, there has been a more lenient attitude toward this problem than in ancient oriental society. The older man was always to be treated with respect. Elisha left Jericho and was traveling to Bethel, a distance of about twenty miles to the west. On the way he was met by a gang of young hoodlums. They were not little children; they were adolescents. Rather than being revered, the prophet became the butt of their distasteful taunting. It has been suggested that the term "baldhead" referred to a peculiar way in which the prophets clipped their hair, rather than to a condition of baldness. The question remains as to how one's head could be seen, considering the headdress worn in the Middle East. Elisha rightfully pronounced upon them that which the Law implied to disrespect of an elder. In a sense, a prophet was to be revered as a father, and thus the injunction of the fifth commandment was applicable. Consequently, God Himself sent judgment upon them. Two female bears tore the young people apart. Bears were common in Palestine at one time, although

1. John Gray, *I and II Kings*, p. 477.

now their habitat seems mainly narrowed to the remote highlands of the Lebanon range. This incident was a divine acknowledgment that Elisha was God's servant.

THE VICTORY OVER MOAB (3:1-27)

The problem of Moab's rebellion, which occurred during Ahaziah's brief reign, became the responsibility of the new Israelite king, Jehoram. Showing some improvement over his father Ahab and his brother, he did take steps to remove the destructive influences of Baal worship. But as his predecessors, he continued the worship system instituted by Jeroboam.

Moab, the principality east of the Jordan, had been ruled by a deputy during Ahab's reign. A Moabite had been reinstituted king as a result of the rebellion during Ahaziah's reign. Moab's rebellion did not affect only Israel. Moab was also a threat to the kingdom of Judah. As his father before him had done, Jehoram enlisted the assistance of Jehoshaphat and also the king of Edom, whose interest in the campaign would be the protection of his northern borders. Traveling seven days into the wilderness of Moab, Jehoram and the other kings were evidently hopeful of finding ample oases to quench the thirst of their armies and their livestock. Jehoram made the first pronouncement regarding their desperate situation: "The LORD has called these three kings to give them into the hand of Moab" (v. 10). This verse demonstrates the fact that Israel's religion, though a distortion of the revealed worship of Jehovah, was not a repudiation of that worship. But distortion can often be more dangerous than outright denial.

Jehoshaphat's response was similar to that which he uttered in the presence of Ahab (1 Kings 22:7): "Is there not a prophet of the LORD here?" One of Jehoram's servants mentioned that Elisha was available. His presence with them in the wilderness was remarkable except for the fact that the Lord brought him there at that time to fulfill His bidding. Elisha was hesitant to act in behalf of this venture. Only because of Jehoshaphat did he agree to consult the Lord.

The message fron Jehovah follows in verses 16-20. The Lord would not only supply the needed refreshment of water, but He would also bring a great victory to the three-king alliance. He further instructed them to destroy the cities and the water systems. Digging trenches as instructed, the people of Israel, Judah, and Edom were witnesses of the powerful hand of Jehovah who provided water without wind or rain.

The Moabites prepared for battle, and early the next morning stood on high ground at their border. As the sun's first rays beamed toward the trenches of the invaders, the Moabites mistakenly believed the reflections they saw to be blood, and that no doubt their adversaries had turned on one another in that desolate and forbidding desert. So now, they thought, it was no longer a matter of battle, but only the collection of booty left on the field. But their arrival at the scene was indeed met with the horror of battle, and the Moabites fled back across their borders with their invaders close behind.

As they had been commanded, the Israelite king and his army laid waste the land. Even a regrouped force of special Moabite troops was unsuccessful in its attempt to block the juggernaut as it rolled through their land. At this point the king of Moab decided on an extreme measure. He sacrificed his firstborn to the Moabite god Chemosh. This act so unnerved the Israelites that they left Moab and returned to their own countries.

## THE PROPHET'S MINISTRY TO WOMEN (4:1-37)

Though the Law made provisions for women of which other nations knew nothing, even in Israel women were considered inferior. So for God to send both Elijah and Elisha to women is indicative not of the prophets' natural bent, but of divine direction. In this section there were two such women, and in each case Jehovah graciously met their needs.

## The impoverished widow (4:1-7)

The first instance of the prophet's ministry to women involved the widow of one from the prophetic guild. When her husband died, she was in debt, and the creditor was about to take her two children as payment. She pleaded with Elisha to help her. From a small amount of oil, the prophet miraculously provided enough oil to pay the debt as well as to meet her needs and those of her two sons.

## The Shunammite woman (4:8-37)

Seemingly at the opposite end of the economic spectrum was a woman of Shunem who had a husband and ample property, but no child. In addition, her husband seemed to be too old to produce an heir. But this woman had provided hospitality for the prophet even to the extent of reserving a special guest room for him. Elisha, expressing his desire to reward her for her kindness, learned that her one simple desire in life was to have a son. Summoning her, Elisha announced that she would become pregnant, and though the idea was incredible to her, her desire was granted.

The chronicler did not stop with that, however. He continued the account by recording the subsequent illness and death of the child. The Shunammite woman placed the inert body of her child in the prophet's room and went to speak with him. She had but a short distance to travel west to the area of Mount Carmel, and there she told the prophet what had happened. Elisha instructed Gehazi, his servant, to go to Shunem and place the prophet's staff on the face of the boy. Elisha and the Shunammite followed. But Gehazi returned to them to announce that his treatment had been ineffective.

Elisha entered the room, recognized that the youngster was dead, and then shut the door. He began with prayer to Jehovah; then he stretched out on the boy, and the child recovered. So the woman of Shunem was called, and she received her son back to life.

### THE PROPHET'S MINISTRY TO HIS DISCIPLES (4:38-44)

The sons of the prophets were probably students of the Law as well as those whose lives were devoted to ministering to their leader. The prophet Elisha returned to Gilgal and ordered the preparation of a stew. One of his servants had gathered wild gourds. When the stew was prepared, a number of them ascertained that the stew was poisonous. Elisha took meal and threw it into the pot, and the stew became edible.

The second miracle was again one of continuing supply. Twenty barley loaves and fresh ears of grain were hardly enough to feed the assembly at Gilgal. But Elisha promised that there would be enough, and some would be left over. This miracle was a prelude to that which Jesus Christ did in feeding both five thousand and four thousand with little.

### THE PROPHET'S MINISTRY TO A SYRIAN (5:1-27)

Probably one of the best-known accounts from the books of the Kings is the one about a Gentile who contracted leprosy and was healed. The central character in the episode was a Syrian army officer named Naaman. The particular period of this narrative is not given. It is noted, however, that he was decorated for his valor and action in bringing victory to Syria. Could he possibly be that mysterious figure in 1 Kings 22:34 who "drew his bow at random and struck the king of Israel in a joint of the armor"?

The character of the times was one of respite between wars. An Israelite girl whom the Syrians had taken prisoner was serving in Naaman's home. She spoke of a prophet in Israel who could heal the soldier. Naaman took his case before the king who, in turn, authorized his going on to Israel. Israel's king, who was probably Jehoram, considered the matter threatening. But

Elisha heard of the problem and sent word to the king to direct Naaman to him.

When the Syrian retinue arrived, Elisha merely sent a messenger who delivered the succinct word, "Go and wash in the Jordan seven times, and your flesh shall be restored to you and you shall be clean." But Naaman had not expected this. He had envisioned a personal confrontation with the prophet followed by some kind of frantic, magic-inducing incantations. Would the prophet send him to the Jordan, when he had left behind him the bubbling, clear waters of the mountain streams of Abanah and Pharpar? Fortunately, he had servants who thought more clearly than he, and they reminded him that he had not been asked to do some great thing. If he had, he would have responded by doing it. Why not do the simple act requested? Accepting such exhortation, the soldier washed and was cleansed.

With a deep sense of gratitude, he returned to Elisha and attempted to pay him. The prophet refused. So Naaman asked a very strange thing. He requested two mules' loads of earth to take back to Syria, where evidently he would use it to make an altar for making sacrifice to Jehovah. He was told to go in peace, but Elisha's servant seized the opportunity for personal gain. He fabricated a lie, and Naaman delivered what he asked. When the servant returned to Elisha, he was faced with his sin and judged with the transfer of Naaman's leprosy to himself and his descendants.

### THE PROPHET'S CONCERN FOR PROPERTY (6:1-7)

Possibly increasing numbers of disciples at the prophet's residence was the reason for the following incident. Additional housing was needed and Elisha's followers volunteered to do the work themselves. In the process of cutting down trees, an axe head fell into the river. Bemoaning the fact that the tool was not only lost but was borrowed as well, the worker appealed to Elisha. After asking where it had fallen, the prophet cast a piece of wood into the river, and the axe head floated. A matter of interest is Elisha's command to the anxious workman to reach out and grab the tool. Elisha, as God's prophet, performed the miracle, but the worker was included in the process of recovery.

### ELISHA AND THE SYRIAN INVASIONS (6:8—7:20)

Two Syrian, or Aramaean, invasions of Israel are noted here. The exact time of these is impossible to pinpoint, and whether the organized Syrian army was involved in both is difficult to ascertain. It seems that the first incident involved marauding bands of Syrians who made border raids against the Jews. The latter probably involved the organized military forces.

### *Deliverance at Dothan (6:8-23)*

The target of the first incident was primarily Elisha and secondarily the king. The prophet had been warning the king of Israel (probably Jehoram) of the location of the Syrian encampments. The king of Syria thought he had security problems among his own soldiers, but he was informed of the powers of Elisha who "tells the king of Israel the words that you speak in your bedroom."

As a result, a considerable force gathered at Dothan where, it had been learned, the prophet dwelled. Assembling under cover of darkness, the army was discovered by Elisha's servant who warned the prophet of what he believed was impending doom. Elisha merely prayed that his servant might have his eyes opened to see what the prophet saw. Elisha's attendant then viewed the host of the Lord assembled for battle.

The prophet now requested that the Syrians be struck with blindness. The request was granted, and Elisha led them into the Israelite capital, Samaria, where their eyes were opened. This sudden turn of events frustrated Israel's leader. He asked if he should slaughter them. But Elisha's reply was in keeping with New Testament truth, "If your enemy hungers, feed him; if he thirsts, give him something to drink" (Rom 12:20, author's trans.). The Syrian invaders were then sent home, and for a time the borders enjoyed a respite from raids.

## Deliverance at Samaria (6:24—7:20)

The invasion of Samaria was much more serious. Again precise dates are not given, but the name of the Syrian king, Benhadad, must refer to Ben-hadad II. Hazael succeeded Benhadad II by murdering him. The date of Hazael's accession to power in Syria was about 844 B.C.

The siege of Samaria had precipitated horror unprecedented in Israel's history. Cannibalism became a means of survival. The grisly record recounts the actions of two women who entered into a bizarre agreement to boil their sons on successive days. When this was reported to the king, he, in anger, placed the blame on the prophet Elisha and vowed to behead the new "troubler of Israel."

So the king sent a messenger for Elisha, but Elisha had been given prior knowledge of the plot. When the messenger arrived, Elisha delivered a message from the Lord that must have been totally confusing to the king's servant. Elisha prophesied the end of the siege of Samaria and, in addtion, abundance of food. When the message was received as an incredible one, Elisha predicted, "You shall see it with your own eyes, but you shall not eat of it" (7:2).

The scene shifts to four lepers—outcasts who were strange observers of these events. The lepers could have entered the city but would have gained nothing in doing so. In fact, as they considered their situation, they realized the possibility of imminent death. They decided to head for the Syrian camp. There they would find food, or, should the Syrians decide to kill them, they would be delivered from death by starvation. The odds were in favor of their choice.

But the four lepers were hardly ready for the sight spread out before them. They gazed in wonder at a military camp that had been quickly vacated. The tents still stood, the livestock stood or grazed under the fading light, but the camp was desolate. Not a Syrian remained. They had fled because God had caused them to hear the sound of a mighty army of chariots and horses. Fearing imminent attack, they had taken flight.

Hardly able to believe what they were observing, the four lepers ran from one tent to another, eating, drinking, and hiding clothing and precious metals. But as the evening wore on, they realized that they could not possibly eat or hide all that the Syrians had left behind, and they returned to the city to tell the king. Fearing some trick by the Syrians, the king sent a small squad to reconnoiter the camp area. Their report was affirmative—the lepers had indeed spoken the truth, and the evidence of the Syrian retreat was littered all the way to the Jordan River.

In a miraculous way Jehovah had delivered his faithless people from the hand of the enemy. Elisha's prophecy that the siege would be lifted and food would become plentiful was fulfilled. But what about the prediction made to the king's servant in 2 Kings 7:2? The last verse of the chapter recounts his death as a result of the sudden breakout of the besieged people when the gates were opened. The unbelieving officer saw but did not partake.

RESTORATION OF LAND TO THE SHUNAMMITE (8:1-6)

Warned by Elisha of impending famine in the land, the Shunammite woman whose devotion to the prophet was so dominant in an earlier chapter, appeared again. The account seems to be out of chronological order for it appears that Elisha had died, and his old servant Gehazi was reviewing the events of the prophet's life. As he was recounting the raising of the widow's son from death, she appeared in the court to appeal to the king that her vacated property be returned to her. Questioning her regarding her experience with the prophet, the king was satisfied, and ordered the property restored.

### ELISHA'S PREDICTION TO HAZAEL (8:7-15)

Hazael's rise to power was predicted to Elijah during his attempt to escape the wrath of Jezebel (1 Kings 19:15). Hazael appears at this point only as a servant of Ben-hadad II. Having been sent to inquire of Elisha concerning the Syrian monarch's sickness, Hazael was furnished information he had hardly expected. His simple inquiry related to the seriousness of Ben-hadad's illness. "Will he recover?" Hazael asked. Elisha replied that though Ben-hadad would recover, he would still die, and the prophet pointed the finger at Hazael. He then prophesied that Hazael would force a bloody coup d' état.

The servant returned to the bedside of his master to announce that the king would recover. Since Hazael was already informed that he was to become king, he decided to hasten the process by murdering his master. He put him to death by suffocation and became the new regent. Hazael's rise to the throne was mentioned in Assyrian records which refer to him as "the son of a nobody." His feigned humility (v. 13) shows the hypocrisy of the man; he attempted to hide his murderous ambitions. A great contrast can be seen between Hazael and David: David waited for God's time to come to power, whereas Hazael decided to advance himself in his own time.

### THE CONTEMPORARY EVENTS IN JUDAH (8:16-29)

#### *The reign of Joram (8:16-23)*

Elisha's saga is interrupted for comment on the events occurring in Judah. The reign of Judah's Jehoshaphat brought him into contact with Ahab, Ahaziah, and Joram (Jehoram) of Israel. Jehoshaphat's death is recorded in 1 Kings 22:50. His foolish alliance with Ahab would bear fruit in the reign of the new

Judean king who had married Athaliah, Ahab's and Jezebel's daughter. The idolatrous practices instituted by them spread like a cancer to Judah. God granted a stay of execution because of His regard for David and for the covenant promises made to him (see Psalm 89:30-37).

Joram of Judah ruled during a time of upheaval. Both Edom and the Philistine city of Libnah revolted, and as was true of Moab to the east, these two countries gained independent status. This situation politically isolated Judah. She became an island surrounded on all sides with trouble. The phrase "to this day" in 8:22 refers to the fact that Edom in its entirety was never again under the domination of Judah.

## The reign of Ahaziah (8:24-29)

Joram's successor, Ahaziah, was his son by Athaliah. His reign was short-lived, however. Continuing the alliance with Israel, he engaged his troops in battle with those of his brother-in-law. Joram of Israel was wounded in the fray and returned to Jezreel to recover. There the Judean king visited him. But the events that occurred at this point revolved around a new dynasty to be established in Israel.

### JEHU ANOINTED AS KING (9:1-13)

The last official act of Elisha was to be of great significance for both Israel and Judah. As in the case of Hazael, Jehu's accession to the throne was predicted to Elijah (1 Kings 19:16). Although Elijah was given the order to anoint Jehu, this task seems to have been part of the unfinished work left to Elisha. Even Elisha did not personally carry out the assignment, but commissioned one of his disciples to do the actual anointing.

Jehu was one of the captains of the northern army (9:5). He was the son of a man named Jehoshaphat, who is not to be confused with the king of Judah bearing the same name. Elisha's servant called Jehu aside, anointed him, and declared to him Jehovah's word concerning what he had done. His rise to the throne was an act of judgment against the house of Ahab. He would be God's instrument to exterminate Ahab's family and to remove Baalistic influences from Israel.

In verses 11-13, Jehu told his fellow soldiers the words of the prophet's servant, and they proclaimed the tidings, "Jehu is king!"

## SUMMARY

To say Elisha's ministry does not seem to have had the political impact of Elijah's is probably misleading. He had an important ministry with individuals and with his students (the sons of the prophets), and his influence politically was, in fact, as dramatic as that of his predecessor. The counsel in battle against Moab, the international extent of his prophetic ministry with Naaman, Ben-hadad, and Hazael, and his direct action in the overthrow of the evil influence of the Omride Dynasty are all evidence of the wide ministry to which he was called. Although no great musical works have been composed to memorialize him, and although he does not appear in many New Testament references, the impact of Elisha's life on his society is forcefully bared to the student who analyzes it. Here indeed was a man who had a double spirit of that remarkable prophet Elijah.

# 6

# Israel's Decline and Disaster

## 2 Kings 9:1–17:41

Elisha's death has not yet been noted at this point, but the prophet faded into obscurity following the anointing of Jehu as Israel's new monarch. It is well to take a moment here to review some of the chronology. The last important date noted was 931 B.C., the year the nation was divided into two kingdoms. With the death of Jehoram of Israel, the Omride Dynasty came to a bloody end. Only the question of Jezebel and the problems of Athaliah in Judah remained unsettled. Jehu came to the throne in 841 B.C. His dynasty, the most enduring in the Northern Kingdom, ended in 753 B.C., only thirty-one years before Israel fell to the invaders of Assyria. Those last thirty-one years were characterized by division within the land as leaders conspired against one another. The effect was bound to be one of great distress and depression for the people.

### THE DYNASTY OF JEHU

### 2 Kings 9:1—14:29

During the eighty-eight-year tenure of Jehu's family, the fortunes of Israel were directed by five kings. Of these, the most effective was Jeroboam II. His long, forty-one year rule and his creative government policies gave a period of stability to the frustrated citizens of the north. But his successes were hardly permanent as is evident in tracing the course of this period.

THE RULE OF JEHU (9:1—10:36)

Elisha was sent to Ramoth-gilead near the northeastern border of Gad's allotted territory of the Jordan. This area was vulnerable to attacks from marauding bands of foreigners as well as to a concerted invasion from an organized army. Jehu was there because of the military situation. As was noted in the last chapter, Elisha not only had the king anointed but delivered a stern commission to him as well. Following the celebration of Jehu's rise, the new ruler turned his thoughts to the charge given to him.

*The assassination of Joram (9:17-26)*

King Joram had been in the same location as his captain, but had returned across the Jordan to Jezreel. This city was at the north end of the Valley of Jezreel and was in the tribal territory of Issachar near Mount Gilboa. He had retreated because of wounds he had suffered in the engagement with Hazael's forces (see 8:29). Jehu, knowing how rapidly news of a coup could be disseminated, gave orders that no one was to leave Ramoth-gilead. He then departed with a force of his supporters and, because of his great haste to precede any news of his rise to power, Jehu gained a reputation as a wild driver.

The watchmen of Jezreel, seeing the approach of his company, sent out a messenger. The man did not return and, as the dust clouds rose higher, another was dispatched. He too was detained. Only when the party could be identified, did King Joram leave in his chariot to meet his captain. Accompanying him was his Judean ally, Ahaziah. They met Jehu at the notorious vineyard area of Naboth, that property gained by Ahab's family through the cunning of Jezebel.

Jehu minced no words about his purpose, and announced that his journey was not one of peace. His reply to Joram's inquiry, "What peace, so long as the harlotries of your mother Jezebel and her witchcrafts are so many?" gripped the Omride king with fear. His last words were a warning to Ahaziah, who fled in his chariot.

Before Joram had time to mount his own chariot and flee, Jehu, with great force, shot him with an arrow. Before Jehu began the chase of Ahaziah, he gave command concerning the disposition of Joram's body. Jehovah had commanded that his body be thrown on that ill-gotten property that had been Naboth's. Thus the blood of Naboth was avenged.

## The assassination of Ahaziah (9:27-29)

Ahaziah evidently tried to make his way to the chariot city of Megiddo. Its great walls would have furnished him refuge if he had reached them. But the archers of Jehu caught up with Ahaziah before he could reach safety and, rather than Megiddo's becoming his place of security, it became the site of his death.

## The death of Jezebel (9:30-37)

The second part of Jehu's commission was the charge to put Jezebel to death. When Jezebel heard Jehu was coming, she painted her face. It seems strange that Jezebel would worry about cosmetics when her life was endangered. Her opening remark is evidence that she was aware of his coup d' état. "Is it well, Zimri, your master's murderer?" (9:31). She was about to die, but she linked Jehu with the assassin of the house of Baasha. A few of Jezebel's servants were loyal to Jehu and obeyed his command to throw her out the window to the courtyard below. The mounted group then trampled her. Disfigured by the horse's hooves, the queen was then chewed by dogs until little of her remained.

## The extermination of the Omride family (10:1-11)

Faced with the need to secure his kingdom, Jehu prepared to eradicate all heirs to the throne. The new king went about his extermination with creativity. First he challenged the guardians of the seventy sons of Ahab to set up one son as heir apparent and to fight for the throne. They refused, knowing how Jehu had already done away with Joram and Ahaziah. They instead proposed servitude to the new king. An embassy from Ahab's house pledged loyalty to Jehu and promised to carry out his orders. Those orders called for the beheading of the family members. The heads were then piled up before the gate. The pile of heads bore somber evidence of the fulfillment of Jehovah's word.

## The slaughter of Ahaziah's relatives (10:12-14)

As he traveled southward in his mission of destruction, Jehu encountered a large caravan of travelers who identified themselves as members of Ahaziah's family. Unaware of the events that had transpired, they were easy prey for Jehu's forces. Jehu killed forty-two men. Obviously, this did not threaten the throne of David that God had promised to sustain.

## The destruction of Baal worship (10:15-28)

Baal worship had thrived for many years under the watchful direction of Ahab and his successors. The victory won through Elijah's contest on Mount Carmel had been only temporary. It was Jehu's clever scheme that finally rid Israel of its heinous practices. Feigning allegiance to Baal, Jehu declared a great celebration for the worship of the so-called "lord of heaven." By furnishing clothing for all the worshipers, Jehu provided easy targets for the weapons of his forces. Attacking the worshipers in their solemn devotion, Jehu's soldiers slaughtered them and smashed their sacred objects. The worship of Baal became a matter of history not to be repeated in Israel.

## The decline of Jehu (10:29-36)

In his twenty-eight-year reign, Jehu was unexcelled in his zeal to rid his people of Baal. But he was reticent to lift a hand against the continued false worship instituted by Israel's first king. The compromise of idol worship combined with the worship of Jehovah still plagued the people of Israel. But Jehu had carried out

God's word of judgment upon the house of Ahab. For that reason, Jehu's heirs would occupy the throne through four generations.

Because of his failure to honor the Lord, however, Jehu was plagued with problems from outside his realm. The king of Syria, Hazael, continued to threaten the northeastern regions of his domain, and piece after piece of real estate came under Syria's domination. Though not mentioned in the text, the famous Black Obelisk discovered in 1846 reveals that Assyria under Shalmaneser III received tribute from Jehu. Hazael's desire to delay an invasion by the Assyrians probably precipitated his action, since he was essentially caught in a vise between Assyria and Israel. The occupation of Israel's northeastern borders may indicate also a lack of unity that festered into an open sore during the last days of the Northern Kingdom.

## CONCURRENT EVENTS IN JUDAH (11:1—12:21)

### *The reign of Athaliah (11:1-21)*

One queen ruled in Judah amid nineteen scions of the house of David. Athaliah was the daughter of the infamous Ahab and Jezebel and was the proponent of Baal worship in Judah. Coming to Judah in a marriage alliance, she established a power base during her husband Jehoram's rule and continued to exert such during the brief reign of her son Ahaziah. At his death, Athaliah took immediate action to exterminate the entire royal family. She would have been remarkably successful too had it not been for Jehosheba, Ahaziah's sister and aunt to the royal children. Jehosheba is a heroine of Scripture, for she boldly took the young infant Joash and protected him from the slaughter. He remained hidden for six years.

But the queen mother, Athaliah, was in virtual control, and though the Bible is silent about her six years of rule, one can imagine the ways in which she pursued her practice of Baal worship. The true worshiper of Jehovah would probably have been sought out and disposed of without much thought. She could hardly have remained ignorant of the violent reforms of Jehu to the north, and this may have led her to great zeal in the encouragement of this false system.

Then a hero emerged—a priest named Jehoiada, the husband of Jehosheba. He was chief minister and, possibly, teacher of the secluded crown prince during this time, and he awaited his opportunity. His tenure of office as priest had extended through the reforms of Asa and Jehoshaphat. Summoning the palace guards, he took them to the house of the Lord, and together they plotted the overthrow of Athaliah. The strategy called for the coup to take place on the Sabbath at the changing of the guard. Elaborate steps were taken to insure the security of the king by furnishing him with an ample bodyguard and protecting the gates through which a counterforce might come. To enforce the sobriety of the occasion, the priest furnished weapons from King David's arsenal to the captains of the guard. Such action would be akin to allowing a concert violinist the use of the finest Stradivarius instrument. It would lend an air of great excitement and intensity to the entire scene.

When the guard had assembled, the young prince was brought out, anointed, and proclaimed king. One must wonder what thoughts transpired in the mind of that seven-year-old boy. After the solemn coronation ceremony, the group erupted in shouts of "Long live the king!" This attracted the attention of Athaliah who had but to follow the noise of the tumult to the Temple area. There she was greeted by the sight of the new monarch standing "by the pillar," the place reserved for royalty. In spite of her protests ("Treason! Treason!"), she was taken out of the Temple area to the stable entrance of the royal palace and executed.

Now that the major supporter of Baal worship was gone, Jehoiada led the citizenry in a great concerted action to rid the country of the objects and persons associated with the Baal cult. Then he turned to the reorganization of the house of God, for its importance to the people had fallen into insignificance since the death of Jehoshaphat (848 B.C.) almost fourteen years before.

### The reign of Joash (12:1-21)

The boy-king came to the throne in troubled times. The character of the society in which he came to power did not change a great deal, but his rule extended over a forty-one-year period. Politically, the Syrians under Hazael continued to affect both the Northern and the Southern Kingdoms. Assyria was growing in power as well. The one thing that probably saved Israel and Judah from greater pressure from Assyria was the instability of her government. This is observed in the repeated notations of revolt that appear in the Assyrian Eponym Lists.[1]

Under the godly direction of Jehoiada, the first official acts of the young king were particularly related to religious improvement. The high places, however, were allowed to remain. This seems to have been a persistent problem, but was not deemed of great importance to change. Or perhaps, the reinstitution of the Temple worship was considered to be of such paramount importance that other problems were given a much lower priority.

The reforms Joash initiated in the early years of his reign were revivalistic. His major reform movement was directed toward the reparation of the Temple. The first measure adopted was the collection of money from the people as freewill gifts to restore the Temple. This plan seemed to have been unsuccessful, so in his twenty-third year of rule, a new procedure was devised. A box was constructed and placed at the right side of the altar of burnt offering. All offerings placed in this box were used for repairing the house of God. The recorder was careful to point out that the coinage collected was not used for any gold or silver utensils of worship (v. 13). The collected funds were used strictly for needed items and for the labor used in refurbishing. Verses 15

---

1. Edwin R. Thiele, *The Mysterious Numbers of the Hebrew Kings*, p. 210. Note especially the years 828-23 B.C.

and 16 note there was neither need for accounting nor misuse of funds. Probably one of the best confirmatory signs of real revival is found in the rebirth of integrity.

The "guilt-offering" of verse 16 is to be distinguished from the "sin-offering" not only by the difference in sacrifices required, but principally by the restitution involved in the guilt-offerings. The addition of one-fifth to the indebted amount was to portray the seriousness of the transgression. An interesting parallel is that used by the apostle Paul in Romans 5:12-21 in which he notes that Jesus Christ became a trespass, or guilt, offering. It is significant indeed that He is the sin-offering, but Paul's emphasis in Romans 5 is that He not only returned what Adam lost but also added to that a restitutive portion.

At this point, the editor includes a note on the military successes of the Syrian king, Hazael (vv. 17-18). Hazael had successfully crossed into the heart of Israel and proceeded down the coast to the Philistine stronghold of Gath. This placed the threat at the gates of Judea, and even Jerusalem was threatened. To ward off the designs of Hazael on the city of the Great King, Joash* offered tribute from the treasuries of the Temple as well as of the palace. This placated Hazael. He left Jerusalem, and that threat was over.

But the reign of the boy-king Joash was not remembered for total religious fervor. With the death of the priest, Jehoiada, which certainly occurred sometime after the twenty-third year of Joash's reign (cf. 12:6-7), Joash led the people of Judah into a spiritual decline. The apostasy is recorded in 2 Chronicles 24:17-27. Abandoning the worship of Jehovah, they turned again to the idolatries of the past. They refused to listen to God's prophets. Joash the king was directly responsible for the death of Jehoiada's son. Judah's forces were beaten by a very small Syrian force, and the servants of Joash murdered him. Thus were fulfilled the

---

*The change in form of the name Joash to Jehoash probably represents a varied source for this series of events.

dying words of Zechariah, the son of Jehoiada, "May the LORD see and avenge."

## THE REIGNS OF JEHOAHAZ AND JEHOASH (13:1-13)

### *The reign of Jehoahaz (13:1-9)*

The second of four monarchs in the family of Jehu was Jehoahaz. He came to the throne of Israel in the same year Joash of Judah initiated his famous offering box. The year was 814 B.C., and this son of Jehu was to reign during a troubled time for seventeen years. Continuing the religious system devised by Jeroboam, he was to reap the judgment of God. In verse 3 an important note is made: Hazael's rule ended, and the new Syrian king was Ben-hadad. Hazael's death probably occurred near 800 B.C. when Ben-hadad II assumed power. Thus for just a few years the new leader of Syria was threatening Jehoahaz.

The king of Israel in desperation called upon the Lord for help, and a deliverer for Israel appeared. The identity of the "deliverer" is not specified. Some have identified him with the new king of Assyria, Adad-nirari (810-783 B.C.). This king invaded Syria in the fifth year of his reign. This action would have placed the deliverance in 805 B.C., clearly within the time of Jehoahaz's rule but before Ben-hadad II came to the throne. By this time Hazael had been ruling for almost forty years, and it is conceivable that the reference in verse 3 was to a coregency established with his son.

But Jehoahaz, as former kings, failed to see that the worship established by Jeroboam was a distortion of the true worship of Jehovah. The false system continued, and is a reminder again that truth that is distorted, but appears to be truth, can be more damaging than outright denial of truth. This fact is evident in that Israel was able to break cleanly with the worship of Baal, but persisted in the merged religion of Jeroboam.

When Jehoahaz ended his rule, his military forces were terribly

deficient. Fifty horsemen, ten chariots, and ten thousand in-
fantrymen could hardly be called even a token force. The chronicler reiterated the terrible price of apostasy.

*The reign of Johoash and the death of Elisha (13:10-25)*

Coming to power at the death of his father, Jehoash (Joash)
ruled Israel for sixteen years. During his first three years, Israel
and Judah had kings with the same name. For twelve of the sixteen years, he shared the rule with Jeroboam II. Little is said of
him in the scriptural account. But the fact that the declining
power of Israel was turned around is evident in 2 Chronicles 25:
17-24 where Jehoash is said to have launched a successful campaign against Amaziah of Judah.

The account in 2 Kings does not mention that campaign against
Amaziah but, in connection with the last days of Elisha, Jehoash's
successes over the Aramaeans as well as the Moabites are recorded. Elisha's influence was evidently minimized during the
reigns of Jehu and Jehoahaz, although an account of his death is
given. Hearing of Elisha's fatal illness, Jehoash went down to
see him and wept and cried, "My father, my father, the chariots
of Israel and its horsemen!" This strange statement was that
which Elisha had uttered as his mentor had been taken away from
him (2 Kings 2:12). It has been estimated that at his death, the
prophet was eighty-five or ninety years old. Possibly Jehoash
expected to see Elisha taken up as Elijah had been. But the aged
prophet's thoughts were not of his departure but of his disobedient
people.

The prophet instructed the king to shoot an arrow. This sig-
nified, he said, "the LORD's arrow of victory" over Syria. Then
Elisha commanded Jehoash to strike the ground with his arrows.
Three times the king did this, and stopped. Elisha protested that,
rather than three times, the king should have struck the ground
five or six times, thereby guaranteeing complete victory over
Syria.

With this, the venerable old prophet died and was buried. The last miracle associated with Elisha occurred during a Moabite raid into Israel. The Israelites, in the act of burying a man, were surprised by the attack. With no time to complete the burial, they threw the body into Elisha's tomb, and the man revived.

The last record of Jehoash's successes is that of the three prophesied victories he was to have over the Syrians. Fighting against Ben-hadad II, Jehoash recovered territory lost to Hazael during the preceding rules.

### THE REIGN OF AMAZIAH OF JUDAH (14:1-14)

Shortly after Jehoash took over rule in Israel, Amaziah, the son of Joash of Judah, became king. His rule extended for twenty-nine years, and much of it was shared with his son and successor, Azariah. Amaziah began his reign in 796 B.C. The principal reason for introducing Amaziah to this point was to record his defeat by Joash, the Israelite king. This probably indicates that documentation for the record was compiled from Israelite as well as Judahite sources.

Amaziah was recognized as one of Judah's good kings. This does not mean that he was a reformer, but only that he was a Jehovist. He could not be compared to David, says the chronicler, but only to his father Joash. When he avenged the murder of his father by executing his slayers, he showed his obedience to the Law by not putting to death the sons of the conspirators.

Militarily, he extended Judah's control into Edom once again. Second Chronicles 25:6 records the hiring of Israelite troops in this successful venture, but he dismissed them before the battle. Enraged, they returned to their homeland, but they left a path of looting and murder.

Amaziah challenged Israel to war. Jehoash of Israel responded with a proverb about a thistle's requesting a marriage alliance with a cedar of Lebanon. Schultz punned, "Evidently Amaziah did not get the point."[2]

Jehoash defeated the forces of Judah at Beth-shemesh (about fifteen miles west of Jerusalem). He then pursued the defeated army to Jerusalem itself. There he captured the king, destroyed a portion of the wall, and plundered both the royal and sacred treasuries. Thiele places the date of this battle at 792 B.C.[3] His death was recorded (14:17) with the interesting note that he lived for fifteen years after the death of Israel's Jehoash. This, as Thiele has shown, represents an important synchronization of the kings during this period.[4] This strange mention of the fifteen years, unique to the record, may indicate the period in which Amaziah was Israel's prisoner and his son Azariah was on the throne of Judah. Thiele's reconstruction of the chronological data of this period is:

| | |
|---|---|
| Jehoash's invasion of Judah | 792 |
| Capture of Amaziah, accession of Azariah | 792 |
| Death of Jehoash and release of Amaziah | 782 |
| Commencement of Jeroboam's sole reign | 782 |
| Death of Amaziah, beginning of Azariah's sole reign[5] | 767 |

## THE REIGN OF JEROBOAM II (14:15-29)

The fourth of the house of Jehu, Jeroboam II was the Northern Kingdom's outstanding ruler. Sharing, as has been noted, twelve years of a coregency, he ruled over Israel as its sole leader for twenty-nine more years (782-753 B.C.). His father was responsible for the early successes that brought Israel back into prominence.

### Concurrent events in Judah (11:17-22)

The reign of this illustrious monarch bridged the reigns of

2. Samuel J. Schultz, *The Old Testament Speaks*, p. 195.
3. Thiele, p. 86.
4. See the discussion in Thiele, pp. 77-81.
5. Ibid., p. 86.

both Amaziah and Azariah (Uzziah). The account includes a brief resume of Amaziah's death. The conspiracy against him may be traced to his failure to stop the Israelite forces some fifteen years previously. However, for the assassins to have held such a grudge for fifteen years seems highly unlikely. Most probably, the conspiracy was of military origin and was sparked by the maturity of the crown prince Azariah. The fact that Lachish, where the murder took place, was a fortress city, possibly indicates a military plot. Amaziah was returned to Jerusalem where he was evidently given a king's funeral.

## Jeroboam's accomplishments (14:23-27)

Beginning in verse 25, a list of Jeroboam's accomplishments is given. The brevity of the account is a reminder that man's accomplishments outside God's will are not important in the final analysis. In this sense, what is recorded is not history as we view it, but a history of following the will of God.

In this study, it is important to discuss Jeroboam's successes. With territory recovered from the approaches to Hamath to the Sea of the Arabah, Israel's borders were extended to east of the Jordan again. Hamath, located in Syria, was more than 150 miles northeast of the Sea of Galilee. The Sea of Arabah is another name for the Dead Sea. Thus Jeroboam brought the vast Trans-Jordan plateau under subjection to Israel. This not only provided Jeroboam with an influential display of prestige, but it also provided Israel with a military buffer between the capital and invaders from the east. This reaccumulation of territory is noted to have been prophesied by Jonah, undoubtedly the same prophet who was sent on a mission to Nineveh (Jonah 1:1). Jonah's residence at Gath-hepher was a short distance north of Nazareth.

Also during the reign of Jeroboam II the prophet Amos reminisced about the cruelties of Hazael, who attacked and subordinated Israel's eastern frontier (Amos 1:3-5). The restoration of these areas marked a decline in Syrian power under Hazael's son, Ben-hadad II.

Amos turned as well to the internal problems of Israel. At this point he no doubt "left off preaching and turned to meddling."

> Thus says the Lord.
> "For three transgressions of Israel and for four
> I will not revoke its punishment,
> Because they sell the righteous for money
> And the needy for a pair of sandals.
> "These who pant after the very dust of the earth on the head
>     of the helpless
> Also turn aside the way of the humble;
> And a man and his father resort to the same girl
> In order to profane My holy name
> "And on garments taken as pledges they stretch out beside
>     every altar,                             .
> And in the house of their God they drink the wine of those who
>     have been fined" (Amos 2:6-8).

Commenting on this period of Israel's history, Amos further pointed out that living conditions had improved. Citizens now occupied "houses of well-hewn stone" instead of the shacks in which they were forced to live under foreign rulers. But in the midst of luxury, Amos showed great sensitivity to the downtrodden. The accumulation of wealth seems often to be followed by moral degeneracy and spiritual disintegration. Both of these characterized life in the kingdom of Jeroboam.

AZARIAH OF JUDAH BECOMES KING (15:1-7)

In the latter third of his reign in Judah, Amaziah gave way to Azariah. A more extensive section here deals with his reign and accomplishments. Azariah's accession to the throne as sole ruler occurred in 768 B.C. Second Kings 15:1 is one of the puzzling passages dealing with chronology. It is well at this point to think through the explanation by Thiele:

> But the synchronism given for the accession of Azariah is the twenty-seventh year of Jeroboam (II Kings 15:1). If Jehoash died and Jeroboam began to rule in 782/81, which we have seen is definitely the case, and if Amaziah died and Azariah began to rule in 768/67, which we have also seen is clearly the case, then the year 768/67, when Azariah began his reign, is the fifteenth year since Jeroboam began his reign in 782/81. But what, then, is to be done about the synchronism of II Kings 15:1, which states that it was in the twenty-seventh year of Jeroboam that Azariah began his reign? . . . Before rejecting the synchronism of II Kings 15:1 as in error, let us endeavor to ascertain what the historical facts might be that are therein contained.
>
> If 768/67, when Amaziah died and Azariah began to reign, marks both the twenty-seventh year of Jeroboam's reign (II Kings 15:1) and also the fifteenth year of this reign since 782/81 when Jehoash died, it would simply mean that Jeroboam had ruled twelve years jointly with his father before the father died, and that the synchronism of II Kings 15:1, instead of being expressed in terms of Jeroboam's sole reign, is expressed in terms of the beginning of his coregency.[6]

Thiele further points out that Jeroboam dated his reign from that point of coregency, and that 2 Kings 15:8 gives another important piece of information about the reign of Azariah. A computation of the years of his reign demonstrates that he was also involved in a coregency of some twenty-four years before the death of his father. Thus it can be shown that Azariah actually began his reign in 792/91 B.C., which was the fifth year of his father's reign. The explanation for this has already been discussed.[7]

THE REIGN OF ZECHARIAH (15:8-12)

Zechariah's short reign of six months was the crushing blow to the house of Jehu which the Lord had foretold (10:30). Zechariah represented the fourth generation. His reign was characterized by the redundant word concerning these Israelite kings, "And he did evil in the sight of the LORD, as his fathers had done."

## THE FINAL KINGS

### 2 Kings 15:10—17:41

Although references to the kings of Judah (Azariah, Jotham, Ahaz, and Hezekiah) are interspersed in this section, discussion of their reigns follows in the next chapter. This study concentrates on the last years of Israel's rebellious kingdom from 753 to 722 B.C. Only about thirty years remained for the Northern Kingdom.

Perhaps the north was even more shot through with division than the scanty records demonstrate. For instance, accumulating evidence shows that there may have been a division among the people who lived on opposite sides of the Jordan. This is evidenced by the reigns of Pekah and Menahem which present another problem in synchronization. But let us return to the text.

THE REIGN OF SHALLUM (15:10-15)

Shallum's rule was the second shortest reign in Israel's history. He occupied the royal palace for only a month. Shallum's fame was established by the fact that he was the murderer of Zechariah. Something may be significant in the mention that he was a "son of Jabesh." This name belonged to the east-of-the-Jordan area of Gilead, and the incident possibly reflects a growing dissatisfaction with the western part of the kingdom. Shallum's short reign marked the beginning of the end for Israel, which we have dated as 752 B.C. Thiele pinpointed this one-month rule as occurring during the months Adar and Nisan in the early spring of 752 B.C.[8]

## THE REIGN OF MENAHEM (15:14-22)

Menahem represented the founder of the last true Israelite dynasty. He and his son accounted for a twelve-year dynastic reign (752-740 B.C.). Menahem's rise to the throne was motivated by Shallum's violent usurpation of the royal residence. Menahem was from Tirzah, former capital of the Northern Kingdom. This again implies growing hostility between eastern and western factions in the kingdom. Some scholars have conjectured that some difference is indicated by the use of the terms "Ephraim" (western) and "Israel" (eastern).[9]

The Syrian threat had been extinguished, but the weakness of that buffer state opened the way for the Assyrians to move west. The invasion under Pul, the king of Assyria, is recorded in verse 19. The identification of this king has been a matter of difficulty for a number of reasons. First, according to the Assyrian records, there is no listing of a king named Pul. Second, the King James Version's text of 1 Chronicles 5:26 seems to indicate that Pul was an Assyrian king who immediately preceded the illustrious Tiglath-pileser III (sometimes spelled Tilgath-Pilneser): "And the God of Israel stirred up the spirit of Pul king of Assyria, and the spirit of Tiglath-pileser king of Assyria, and he carried them away" (1 Chron 5:26, KJV). Then, according to the older chronology, Menahem came to the throne in 761 B.C. and paid tribute to Pul.[10]

However, in the Assyrian records, Tiglath-pileser III, who came to power in 746/45 B.C., collected tribute from Menahem. In the revised records in which synchronization has been estab-

8. Thiele, p. 88.
9. Mervin Stiles, *Synchronizing Hebrew Originals from Available Records*. Photo reproduction.
10. G. F. Maclear, *A Class Book of Old Testament History*, p. 433.

lished, it has now been definitely shown that (1) Pul and Tiglath-pileser III were the same individual; (2) Menahem came to Israel's throne in 752/51 B.C.,[11] and (3) the Hebrew verb "carried" is singular, thus making the translation in the King James Version grammatically impossible. The problem is clarified by the use of "and" rather than "even" (a permissible act), thus identifying the two names of one individual. It has been further demonstrated that the Babylonians knew him by the name Pul or Pulu and the Assyrians by the name Tiglath-pileser III.

The payment of tribute money to the Assyrian king seemed to diminish any designs he might have had for a wanton overrun of the land. Though the price was high, Israel was safe for the time being.

### THE REIGN OF PEKAHIAH (15:23-26)

Pekahiah's two-year rule began during the fiftieth year of Judah's Azariah (742/41 B.C.). His rule was a continuation of his father's policies, both politically and spiritually. It must be kept in mind that his background was Samarian. He was from the western part of the Northern Kingdom. Thus revolution against him by Pekah would be expected from the eastern schism. Again the Scripture implies this division: "Then Pekah son of Remaliah, his officer, conspired against him and struck him in Samaria, in the castle of the king's house with Argob and Arieh; and with him were *fifty men of the Gileadites,* and he killed him and became king in his place (2 Kings 15:25; itals. added).

### THE REIGN OF PEKAH (15:27-31)

Thiele correctly observes, "The period we are about to enter bristles with difficulties, both internal and external. It is here that the most baffling problems of Hebrew chronology are found."[12]

11. For a full discussion of the problem, see Thiele, pp. 90-93.
12. Ibid., p. 118.

The reign of Pekah was one of the most complex. Why? In the first place, the Scripture records a twenty-year reign for him. If he came to the throne at the death of Pekahiah in 740 B.C., his reign extended two years past the end of the Northern Kingdom. This is impossible. Also, the last king of Israel was not Pekah but Hoshea, who reigned nine years. The most plausible explanation for this problem is that Pekah, the easterner, ruled over the eastern area of Gilead, not as a coregent, but as a contemporary of Menahem and his son Pekahiah.

An allied problem relates to the kings of Judah—Azariah, Jotham, and Ahaz.

Thiele, presenting a chronology for the period, notes that these

are the most important contacts between Assyria and the Hebrews of this period, providing a pattern of years with which the Hebrew years must be in agreement:

| | |
|---|---|
| Appeal by Ahaz to Tiglath-pileser for aid against Pekah and Rezin | c. 734 |
| Attacks by Tiglath-pileser against Philistia, Syria, and Israel | 734-732 |
| Murder of Pekah and Assyrian participation in Hoshea's accession | 732 |
| Three-year siege of Samaria by Shalmaneser V | 725-723 |
| Late claim of Sargon to the capture of Samaria as his reign began | c. 722 |
| Attack by Sennacherib on Judah in the fourteenth year of Hezekiah | 701[13] |

In summary fashion, then, one must note from this data that Pekah came to power in 752 B.C., or in the same year that Menahem successfully overturned the eastern-led rebellion of Shallum. Though details in the scriptural account are lacking, nothing weakens the view that there were growing division and rivalry between the eastern and western Israelite territories.

13. Ibid., p. 120.

THE REIGN OF HOSHEA (17:1-6)

Hoshea was the last king to come to the throne of Samaria. Though "he did evil in the sight of the LORD," his evil was not patterned after that of preceding Israelite kings (v. 2). After the redundant testimony concerning the others, this is a most interesting note. Exactly what it means is not known, although several suggestions have been made. Some believe that political matters were of such magnitude that Hoshea had no time to deal with religious ones. Montgomery asks and then answers,

> Is it a sympathetic expression of this last and valiant king? A Jewish tradition appears in Rashi and Kimchi to the effect that Hoshea removed the guards set on the road to Jerusalem to keep Israelites from going thither to worship.[14]

Hoshea began by honoring the Assyrian power, but then attempted to get out from under its oppressive overlording by making a secret agreement with Egypt. This foolish move resulted in imprisonment for Hoshea, and left Israel without leadership. It also brought the Assyrians into the land like locusts (see Joel 1: 4-7).

Thus in 722 B.C., after a three-year siege, the capital of Samaria lay in ruins, and the people of Israel found themselves deported after a seven-hundred-year occupancy of the land. Someone years ago commented, "God does not pay at the end of every day, but at the end—He pays." All that Moses had foretold came to pass (cf. Deut 28:58-68).

### GOD'S VINDICATION OF HIS JUDGMENT

### 2 Kings 17:7-23

Verses 7-23 comprise God's indictment against Israel. Idolatry is obviously the primary cause. But idolatry left unexplained would be too general a term. Idolatry is really a matter of priori-

14. James A. Montgomery, *A Critical and Exegetical Commentary on the Books of Kings,* p. 465.

ties. Except for the period in which Ahab and Jezebel promoted Baal worship, there seems to have been no period in which the people disavowed belief in Jehovah. Their idolatry was basically a matter of not placing Him in the position required by the first commandment.

These misplaced priorities led to an adoption of the culture around them. They "walked in the customs of the nations whom the LORD had driven out before the sons of Israel" (v. 8). And their apostasy was not confined to themselves; it affected their brothers to the south (v. 19).

Compromise and acceptance of an apostate culture were the principal sins of which God accused His people. Their experience furnishes for all time the reminder that these two sins always lead to spiritual declension.

### THE DEVELOPMENT OF SAMARITAN RELIGION
### 2 Kings 17:24-41

With the deportation of Israel, the Assyrian king ordered new inhabitants into the land. But the Lord did not leave the new inhabitants without difficulties. Though lions had stalked the region before, they seemed to present new and much more difficult problems. The new inhabitants faced more than an ordinary number of attacks, and as a result, they believed that they must accrue some knowledge of the god of that land.

A priest from among the captives was sent back to give instruction, but the result was a compromise system once again. Each of the national groups adapted its religious system to the worship of Jehovah. "They feared the LORD and served their own gods" (v. 33).

The problems encountered by the returning exiles under Nehemiah's leadership (Neh 4:1 ff.), as well as the animosity toward the Samaritans and their false religion reflected in the New Testament (John 4:9), were the direct result of this attempt to be all-inclusive.

# 7

# Recovery, Reform, Relapse, and Ruin

## 2 Kings 14:1—25:30

In the previous chapter, the course of Israel's history was traced. Only incidentally did the Southern Kingdom come to the front stage. In this concluding chapter, Judah's history occupies our attention. The beginning date is traced from Amaziah's accession in 796/95 B.C. through the year of the release of Jehoiachin from prison in about 568 B.C., a period of two hundred years.

## THE REIGN OF AMAZIAH

### 2 Kings 14:1-20

Amaziah's interesting reign was briefly treated in the last chapter. He was noted as one of Judah's good kings, and the student is being reminded that there were only eight. Amaziah was the second in a series of four whose reigns extended until 735 B.C. when the weak monarch Ahaz assumed power. Amaziah's total years as king were twenty-nine, though it should be noted that for eleven or twelve years of that time he was a prisoner in Israel, and his son was the acting regent.

### AMAZIAH'S ACCESSION (14:1-6)

Amaziah was suddenly thrust into power because his father Joash was murdered. After gaining a good hold on the throne, he put his father's murderers to death, but he did not touch their families. Although reckoned as a "good" king, Amaziah was not a reformer. He tolerated religious compromise, and the people continued to burn incense on the "high places."

### AMAZIAH'S WAR AGAINST EDOM (14:7; 2 CHRON 25:1-16)

The chronicler of Kings noted that Amaziah waged a successful campaign against the Edomites, and 2 Chronicles gives the details. The tribes of Judah and Benjamin mustered an army of 300,000 to fight against Edom. The objective was to control the trade routes to the south, especially to the seaport of Elath on the Red Sea.

Possibly considering his force to be almost equal to the objective, Amaziah wanted to tip the scales in his favor, so he hired 100,000 mercenaries from Israel. At this point, God sent a prophet who warned that the Lord would not bless the army of Israel with His presence. When Amaziah expressed worry about the price he had paid, the prophet said God was able to reimburse him many times over. Amaziah sent the mercenaries home, and 2 Kings records the result of the battle. Ten thousand of the enemy were killed. Chronicles adds that another 10,000 were captured, and the objectives were secured.

### AMAZIAH'S DEFEAT AND IMPRISONMENT (14:8-14; 2 CHRON 25:6-25)

The dismissed Israelite mercenaries were angry at not being able to participate. As they returned home northward, they left a trail of pillage and death.

The successes against Edom had a bad effect on Amaziah. He set up Edomite gods and worshiped them (2 Chron 25:14-16). Again a prophet was sent to warn him. Little did he realize how Jehovah's judgment would come. Returning to Judah after his successes, he discovered the wreckage left by the soldiers of Israel. This may have provoked his challenge of King Jehoash of Israel. Jehoash refused at first. In an intimidation attempt, he likened Amaziah to a thorn bush, and himself to a mighty cedar of Lebanon.

But Amaziah was persistent and, without a directive from God, he went into battle. The results were disastrous for Judah. Defeated at Beth-shemesh, Amaziah's troops fled eastward to Jerusalem. The army of Israel captured Jerusalem and destroyed over 600 feet of the city's defensive wall. Amaziah himself was captured. So the king and a considerable amount of booty were carried off to the north. Demoralized, defeated, and depressed, the people of Judah placed Amaziah's son, Azariah, on the throne. A mere youth of sixteen, he guided the destiny of Judah during his father's twelve-year exile.

### AMAZIAH'S DEATH (14:17-20)

Verse 17 notes that Amaziah outlived Jehoash of Israel by fifteen years. This could also indicate the time of Amaziah's release from prison and the resumption of his reign over Judah as coregent with Azariah. But Amaziah was not to die peacefully. He discovered a conspiracy against him and fled to Lachish, but the escape effort was futile. He was killed in Lachish, and Azariah once more found himself solely in charge.

## THE REIGN OF UZZIAH (AZARIAH)

### 2 Kings 14:21-22; 15:1-17

To fully explore the impressive rule of Uzziah, it is necessary to study the parallels in 2 Chronicles 26, where the whole chapter is given to the record of this king. Uzziah is also called Azariah in Scripture.

### UZZIAH'S ACCESSION (14:21; 15:1-4)

The young king evidently came to the throne because his father was imprisoned in Israel. For about twelve years, Uzziah lived with the realization that he was king only for the time being. But the young man did not quail before the responsibility. He was a very active king. He came to the throne in 793/92 B.C., and his reign extended for fifty-two years until 740/39 B.C. He was a good king, though not a reformer. That he may have been considered great can be inferred from a word by his contemporary, Isaiah: "In the year of King Uzziah's death, I saw the Lord" (Isa 6:1).

## UZZIAH'S SUCCESSES (2 CHRON 26:6-15)

The move from 2 Kings 15:4 to 15:5 is abrupt. Uzziah's leprosy might appear to be the result of his failure to deal with the high places, but such was not the case. The record in Chronicles presents a background for his being smitten with leprosy.

Spiritually, Uzziah began well. He continued to ask for divine guidance even into the time of Israel's King Zechariah (754-752 B.C.). Militarily, he rebuilt the Edomite seaport of Elath, carried out successful campaigns against the Philistines, and subdued the Arabians and the Ammonites, thus securing his borders on three sides. He fortified Jerusalem by rebuilding and strengthening the defenses destroyed by Jehoash. The wilderness areas were secured by small fortifications. His army of 307,500 men was commanded by an elite corps of 2,600 officers, and they were furnished with weapons which at that time represented the highest technological advances.

## UZZIAH'S FAILURE AND GOD'S JUDGMENT (2 KINGS 15:5-7;
### 2 CHRON 26:16-21)

Because he had been successful, Uzziah felt that he could move into any area of his kingdom that he might choose. His pride became his captor. Presuming to do the work of a priest, he was intercepted by the high priest and eighty other priests. They warned him that he was out of line with God's directives, and Uzziah was angered by this rebuke. Failing to retreat, he was consequently struck with leprosy and forced to live apart from his subjects. Since this evidently occurred about thirteen years before his death, it would account for the coregency of Jotham, his son (2 Kings 15:5). Though Uzziah may have still guided Judah, he was a leper, and as a leper he died.

## THE REIGN OF JOTHAM

### 2 Kings 15:32-38

This period of time raises further difficult chronology problems. In the succeeding chapters of 2 Kings, there are two separate chronologies, one of which appears to be incorrect. For example, Jotham's reign was dated from Pekah's second year (2 Kings 15:32), and he reigned for sixteen years (2 Kings 15:33). This is in accord with 16:1 which records the time of the accession of Ahaz. But in 2 Kings 15:27, Pekah's reign of twenty years is dated from Azariah's last year, his fifty-second. That would mean that Jotham did not come to the throne until two years after his father's death, an impossibility in light of the record. Because of the nature of this commentary, it would be impossible to develop fully the explanation, and it is unnecessary as well since Edwin Thiele has so masterfully handled it.[1]

### JOTHAM'S ACCESSION (2 KINGS 15:5, 32-35; 2 CHRON 27)

Jotham began his rule while his father was still living (2 Kings 15:5) and he ruled sixteen years. He began his coregency in 752 B.C. and thus was a coregent for twelve of the sixteen years (Uzziah had died in 740 B.C.). That he ruled alone only four years may be indicated in the parallel in 2 Chronicles 27:5, which says that the Ammonites paid tribute to him for a three-year period. The dating of his accession with Pekah rather than with Menahem possibly indicates a strong alliance based on Judah's and Israel's mutual anti-Assyrian policy.

It is understood from Assyrian records that Assyria's power

1. Edwin R. Thiele, *The Mysterious Numbers of the Hebrew Kings*, p. 135.

was beginning to be felt among the western groups of nations. Jotham continued the policies instituted by his father and made impressive by the fine military machine he had developed.

## JOTHAM'S REIGN (2 CHRON 27:2-6)

Jotham's reign was prestigious and successful. Spiritually, Jotham reverenced Jehovah, but he did not remove the high places. This redundancy seems to indicate that such toleration was considered trivial by the individual ruler, although it did not go unnoticed by God. Militarily, Jotham continued to strengthen the nation's defenses. This need was critical because Tiglath-pileser made frequent campaigns to extend Assyrian influence. Jotham's policies seem to have been in accord with those of Pekah of Israel and of Syria (Aram) since there is no record of difficulty with the northern neighbors.

But a strange reference in 2 Kings 15:30 mentions Jotham's twentieth year. This seems an impossibility, because the correct chronology allows him a sixteen-year rule. The problem is solved by a knowledge of the political situation described in 15:29. Tiglath-pileser had turned his attention westward, and in sizeable bites had decimated the Northern Kingdom. We know from Assyrian annals that from 743-738 B.C. and again from 736-732 B.C., the Assyrians moved against the west. The campaign against Urartu in 735 B.C. may have precipitated a chain of events that caused a pro-Assyrian faction to replace Jotham with his weak son, Ahaz. At any rate, Jotham seems to have lived on for four years after what was probably an involuntary retirement.

Second Kings 15:37 would then be explained in terms of the new pro-Assyrian policy in Judah. Whereas Pekah and Jotham had evidently been allies, this relationship changed with the accession of Ahaz. Pekah, along with his Syrian colleague, decided to move against Jerusalem. This is discussed under "The Reign of Ahaz," though Jotham lived to see some of these things begin to emerge.

## THE REIGN OF AHAZ

### 2 Kings 16:1-20

To gain an accurate feeling for this period, one must imagine the situation. Jotham, reigning alone for only four years, was trying to keep his kingdom intact. Syria was threatening from the northeast. Political feelings within Jotham's kingdom were strong, and they unfortunately ran counter to the policies of the king. Only this explains the sudden elevation of Ahaz to the throne. To the detriment of Judah, Ahaz was everything that his father was not. Politically, he was pro-Assyrian; religiously, he was an idolator; administratively, he seems to have been a weakling.

#### THE ACCESSION OF AHAZ (16:1-14)

Gaining the throne in 735 B.C., Ahaz would see momentous events during his reign of sixteen years.

He began to rule with a religious reform in the wrong direction. Not since the reign of Athaliah had Judah's religious life been so affected by a turn in spiritual direction. He was compared to the kings of Israel, but contrasted with them as well. Verse 3 notes that he made his son pass through the fire. This practice was associated with the worship of Molech, the national god of the Ammonites. The significance of the high places, which had long been tolerated, as well as the contacts that Judah had with Ammon, evidently swayed Ahaz. One must reason that the "son" mentioned in verse 3 must not have been the heir apparent, who was obviously Hezekiah.

#### GOD'S JUDGMENT UPON AHAZ (16:5-9)

The judgment of the Lord is not always obvious and direct, but can be subtle. In this section we observe both aspects. The first is the obvious—the invasion of Judah by the confederate armies of Israel and Syria (Aram). The account of the invasion is found in 2 Chronicles 28:5-15. The casualties inflicted upon

Judah were heavy—120,000 dead in a day and 200,000 carried away in captivity. All that remained to be done was the disposition of Ahaz and the setting up of a puppet king. Then the Davidic dynasty would come to an end. This was Judah's darkest hour.

Isaiah, who probably was the chief recorder of this period, gave additional insight into the situation. Ahaz was frightened, and Jehovah instructed Isaiah to bring a message of encouragement. Isaiah was careful to note that the word of God was directed to the king only, as the representative of the house of David. Isaiah 7:4-9 records the Lord's message through the prophet. The threat against Judah would pass. The designs of Pekah and Rezin would "not stand nor shall it come to pass."

Ahaz was pessimistic, and possibly even cynical. He not only disbelieved Isaiah, but he would not ask for a confirmatory sign. Consequently, in the great messianic text of verse 14, Isaiah declared, "Therefore the LORD Himself will give you a sign: Behold, a virgin will be with child and bear a son, and she will call His name Immanuel."

What did this mean to Ahaz? Was Isaiah prophesying about some distant event, or was he speaking of something that Ahaz would see? Or did the prophecy have a double reference? Since this prophecy was to be a confirmatory sign to the house of David, it seems appropriate to take it as a prophecy of double reference. This view is recognized by many commentators as not only possible but required by the context. Fausset wrote:

> Language is selected such as, whilst *partially* applicable to the immediate event, receives its *fullest* and most appropriate and exhaustive accomplishment in Messianic events. . . . the temporary fulfillment is an adaptation of the far-reaching prophecy to the present passing event, which foreshadows typically the great central end of prophecy, Jesus Christ.[2]

2. A. R. Fausset, "Isaiah," in *A Commentary, Critical, Experimental and Practical on the Old and New Testaments* by Robert Jamieson, A. R. Fausset, and David Brown, 3:586.

Other teachers differ, however, and see the prophecy only as a reference to events surrounding the birth of Christ. But if it did have an immediate fulfillment, who was the child? Several suggestions have been given. Some think the child was Ahaz's son, Hezekiah. But by this time Hezekiah was already a youngster at least nine or ten years of age. Contextually, it appears he was the child Maher-shalal-hash-baz, born to Isaiah and his wife (8:3). This seems confirmed by the similarity of events to be fulfilled in the boy's infancy and early childhood (Isa 7:16; cf. 8:4).

Ahaz's idea was to call Tiglath-pileser, king of Assyria, to aid him. The Assyrian responded. Marching westward, he reduced the kingdom of Israel to little more than a tributary of Assyria. Tiglath-pileser replaced Pekah with Hoshea. The Assyrian king was to record, "They overthrew their king Paqaha (Pekah) and I placed Ausi' (Hoshea) as king over them."[3] These events took place in 734-732 B.C. Then Tiglath-pileser turned his attention to the Syrian (Aramean) capital of Damascus. The city fell, and this event precipitated the overthrow of Pekah in 732 B.C.

But the Lord was at work in a subtle way also. According to 2 Chronicles 28:20, Tiglath-pileser "came against him and afflicted him instead of strengthening him." Ahaz himself was brought under the mastery of this ruthless leader.

### AHAZ'S REVOLT AGAINST THE WORSHIP OF JEHOVAH (16:10-18)

To accommodate the Assyrian king, Ahaz decided to remodel the Temple area. He ordered Urijah the priest to erect a new altar and to place it in a prominent position. Until then, this position had been the site of the great bronze altar. Several other changes were made in an attempt to win the favor of the Assyrian lord. These things Ahaz did "because of the king of Assyria" (v. 18). Fortunately, Ahaz's rule was a short one, and his successor brought a brief period of recovery before the nation was plunged headlong into ruin.

3. James B. Pritchard, *Ancient Near Eastern Texts Relating to the Old Testament*, p. 283.

## THE REIGN OF HEZEKIAH
### 2 Kings 18:1—20:21

No king since Solomon is accorded a fuller or a more positive record than Hezekiah. Only two others beside him are said to have done right in the sight of the Lord "according to all that his father David had done" (18:3; cf. 1 Kings 15:11 and 2 Kings 22:2).

Hezekiah came to the throne in 715 B.C. By then the Northern Kingdom was only a memory. Syria was a vassal state; Assyria was riding the crest of empire. Voracious for territory, the Assyrian juggernaut had moved east and west. Sargon II, who took the credit for the conquest of Israel (though that distinction belonged to Shalmaneser V), was on the throne of Assyria. He would not be a threat to Judah. But following his death in battle in 704 B.C., Judah would be much in the Assyrians' thoughts.

### HEZEKIAH'S ACCESSION (18:1-6)

Following the standard formula, Hezekiah is introduced by establishing the date his rule began. At once, we are involved in the chronological difficulty that hopefully was resolved earlier. Using the synchronization suggested by Thiele, Hezekiah assumed power in 715 B.C., approximately seven years *after* the dissolution of the Northern Kingdom. One should exercise caution in becoming dogmatic about this dating. Competent evangelical scholars are not unified regarding this question.*

Hezekiah's rule extended for twenty-nine years. This reign may be divided into two periods: the first, fourteen years; and the second, a fifteen-year period. His rule was characterized not only by devotion to Jehovah, but by devotion of such intensity that finally the high places were destroyed.

---

*Edward J. Young (*The Book of Isaiah* 2:540-42) argues effectively for the use of 2 Kings 18:1 as the clear passage and 18:13 representing the problem. John C. Whitcomb's chart, *Old Testament Kings and Prophets,* as well as Thiele and others, uses 18:13 as the clear reference and feel that 18:1 represents the problem.

We are given insight into another deviation which had caused spiritual deterioration. Moses' brazen serpent (Num 21:6-9) had become an object of worship. Unmentioned for generations, this relic was destroyed. One cannot avoid speculation concerning the din of protest that must have arisen from the "Jerusalem Historical Society" and other such groups. But Hezekiah felt no relic should distort a true conception of the God of Israel.

The verbs used in verses 5 and 6 magnificently highlight this man's consecration. "He trusted in the LORD," "he did not depart from following Him," and he "kept His commandments." This commentary, written after his death, would be an epitaph that any believer in Christ would desire.

### HEZEKIAH'S RELIGIOUS REFORMS (18:3-4; 2 CHRON 29:5—31:21)

The record in Kings does not reveal the extent of Hezekiah's religious reforms. Almost three chapters in Chronicles are devoted to the highlights. He repaired the Temple that had been desecrated during Ahaz's rule. Temple worship was restored and then all Israel, North and South, was invited to the celebration of Passover. The invitation to the remnant of Ephraim and Manasseh (2 Chron 30:1) is further evidence that Hezekiah's reign occurred after Israel's fall.

### HEZEKIAH'S CRISES (18:7—20:11)

*A military crisis (18:13—19:37)*

Hezekiah is a reminder to all who share his faith that trust in God does not result in a problem-free life. In the year 701 B.C., Judah was invaded by Assyria under the leadership of Sennacherib, the son of Sargon II. Sennacherib ruled Assyria from 704-681 B.C. Hezekiah's change in policy from that of Ahaz brought about the invasion. The record of Sennacherib's campaign against Judah was preserved in a series of hexagonal clay cylinders. The text relating to Hezekiah notes that Sennacherib successfully conquered Sidon in Phoenicia, Beth-Dagon in Philistia, and cities in the heartland of the land of Israel. Then he turned to Hezekiah.

> As to Hezekiah, the Jew, he did not submit to my yoke, I laid siege to 46 of his strong cities, walled forts and to the countless small villages in their vicinity, and conquered them by means of well-stamped earthramps, and battering rams brought thus near to the walls combined with the attack by foot soldiers, using mines, breeches as well as sapper work. I drove out of them 200,150 people, young and old, male and female, horses, mules, donkeys, camels, big and small cattle beyond counting, and considered them booty. Himself I made a prisoner in Jerusalem, his royal residence, like a bird in a cage. I surrounded him with earthwork in order to molest those who were leaving his city's gate. His towns which I had plundered, I took away from his country and gave them over to Mitinti, king of Ashdod, Padi, king of Ekron, and Sillibel, king of Gaza.[4]

In an attempt to deter Sennacherib, Hezekiah paid tribute, but this did not seem to sway the Assyrian's determination. Instead, he dispatched three officers with a large force to Jerusalem (18:17). Presumably, Tartan, Rab-saris, and Rabshakeh were not names but titles. Tartan probably was the general of the army, Rab-saris may have been a high military ruler, and Rabshakeh a high civil official.

The strategy utilized was intimidation. The trio implied that all Judah trusted was weak and helpless; help would come neither from the nation's political alliances with Egypt nor from their God, Jehovah. The Assyrian leaders seemed to believe that Hezekiah's removal of Ahaz's pagan altar was a removal of an altar to Jehovah (18:22). They taunted that they would furnish two thousand horses if the beleaguered Judeans could find men to put upon them. Then the promises began: "Submission to

4. Pritchard, p. 288.

Sennacherib will result in a better life, so don't listen to Hezekiah's ravings about trusting in the Lord. No god has stood before the mighty power of Assyria!" (18:32-34, author's paraphrase). The men of Judah answered nothing. Hezekiah's representatives left the wall and reported to the king the ordeal through which they had come.

Hezekiah, in an action characteristic of a man of God, went to the Temple. From there he sent his steward, his scribe, and the priestly leaders to the prophet Isaiah (19:1-2). They had carefully prepared the text of their message to the prophet. It was a message of resignation. All that really remained was to request the prophet to pray for "the remnant that is left" (19:4). Instead, Isaiah gave a message of great hope: the Assyrians would leave the land.

When the Rabshakeh returned to Sennacherib, the Assyrian king was engaged in battle with Judah's ally, Cush of Egypt, whose forces were led by Tirhakah. The appearance of this individual presents another problem. Finegan notes that a Cushite dynasty was ruling Egypt, and this king ruled from 689 B.C. Finegan does not believe the crown prince led the Egyptian troops, because he would have been no more than eight years old. Thus, there must have been two separate campaigns, one recorded in 2 Kings 18:13—19:8 and the other in 19:9-37.[5] But the text does not support such a view since Hezekiah would probably have been gone by the time Tirhakah appeared. The fact that there is a lack of inscriptional evidence makes Archer's case plausible, that is, there was possibly more than one Tirhakeh. He bases his supposition on the redundancy of names in Egyptian annals.[8]

The strategy of intimidation having failed, the Rabshakeh next sent a letter by messengers. The leter again charged Hezekiah with the folly of trusting in the Israelite God. Hezekiah took the letter and placed it before the Lord. The first of two famous

---

5. Jack Finegan, *Light from the Ancient Past,* pp. 212-13.
6. Gleason L. Archer, *A Survey of Old Testament Introduction,* pp. 281-82.

prayers by this king appears in 19:15-19. Hezekiah pleaded for the hand of the Lord to move so "that all the kingdoms of the earth may know that Thou alone, O Lord, art God" (19:19). His prayer was answered through the prophet Isaiah. The answer was a grand expression of the sovereignty of God. "Because Assyria has mocked Zion, in reality she has mocked the Holy One of Israel. The Assyrians have forgotten what history records of Me," the Lord declared, "but I am aware of it, and will force you out of the land" (19:21-28, author's paraphrase).

To Hezekiah, this was confirmed with a sign (19:29). Jamieson noted:

> The "sign" which Isaiah goes on to promise, in terms apparently made obscure in order to excite consideration, seems best explained to mean, that the Assyrian devastations of the open country of the Jews had prevented the regular cropping of the land, and consequently the regular harvest for the current year; and as the enemy was still in occupation of the country, there was no possibility of plowing and sowing, in preparation for the next year either, but the season after that, the prophet confidently asserts that they would be able to sow and reap, and plant vineyards, and eat the fruit thereof.[7]

Faithful to specific conditons of His promise, that very night the angel of the Lord "struck 185,000 in the camp of the Assyrians; and when men rose early in the morning, behold, all of them were dead" (19:35). Finegan mentions an account of Herodotus that describes the defeat of the Assyrians by an invasion of rodents, and he suggests, "Perhaps this is the real explanation of the disaster referred to in II Kings 19:35 as a smiting of the army by an angel of the Lord, for plague and disease elsewhere in the Bible are regarded as a smiting by an angel of God (II Samuel 24:15-17; Acts 12:23)."[8]

7. Robert Jamieson, "Joshua-Esther," in *A Commentary, Critical, Experimental and Practical on the Old and New Testaments* by Robert Jamieson, A. R. Fausset, and David Brown, 2:430.
8. Finegan, p. 214.

*A personal crisis (20:1-11)*

These events would be a terrible strain on the king, and he became "sick to the point of death" (20:1, marginal reading NASB). Neither the exact time this occurred nor the nature of his infliction is stated. That fifteen years were added to his life implies that the sickness was at the time of the Assyrian invasion. When the prophet told Hezekiah to prepare for death, Hezekiah tearfully reviewed his zeal for the Lord (20:3). Isaiah was then instructed to return and tell the king that God would heal him and add fifteen years to his life. As a sign confirming the word from the Lord, the sun's shadow moved backward ten degrees.

### HEZEKIAH'S FOLLY (20:12-20)

His pursuit of an anti-Assyrian policy not only led Hezekiah to alliances with Egypt but with Babylon as well. Babylon represented the most formidable resistance to Assyria. When Hezekiah was ill, the king of Babylon sent Hezekiah presents, as well as letters wishing for his recovery. Hezekiah, attempting to show gracious hospitality to the messengers, showed them all the treasures of his kingdom.

Isaiah appeared and asked three questions: "What did these men say?" "From where have they come?" and "What have they seen in your house?" Hezekiah told all, and Isaiah delivered God's message: the Babylonians would come and take all of it, and some of his sons would be taken captive and serve in the royal offices of Babylon. Hezekiah's response reflected his humanness. Isaiah's prophecy would not affect Hezekiah's kingdom, and the remainder of his years would be years of peace.

### HEZEKIAH'S ACCOMPLISHMENTS AND DEATH (20:20-21)

The successful reign of Hezekiah undoubtedly had many facets that remain unrecorded. But one last accomplishment appears in the picture like a subtle brush stroke. That is the mention of "how he made the pool and the conduit, and brought water into the city" (20:20). This was the most lasting of all his accomplishments. Today, one can wade from the Spring of Gihon to the Pool of Siloam by way of Hezekiah's tunnel, skillfully dug through Jerusalem's bedrock. Unger describes this:

> The intermittent spring of Gihon, Jerusalem's most ancient water supply, was located below the steep eastern hill (Ophel) in the deep Kidron Valley. It was thus exposed to enemy attack. Hezekiah completely covered over this ancient spring and diverted it through a conduit 1777 feet long and hewn out of solid rock into a reservoir within the city walls.[9]

The tunnel became famous when in 1880 an inscription on its walls was discovered. Unger includes the text of the inscription describing the work:

> The boring through is completed. Now this is the story of the boring through. While the workmen were still lifting pick to pick each toward his neighbor and while three cubits remained to be cut through, each heard the voice of the other who called his neighbor, since there was a crevice in the rock on the right side. And on the day of the boring through the stone cutters struck, each to meet his fellow pick to pick; and there flowed the waters to the pool for 1200 cubits and 100 cubits was the height of the rock above the heads of the stone cutters.[10]

In 686 B.C. Hezekiah's fifteen years came to fulfillment. One would have hoped that his young son, who spent the first eleven years of his reign as a co-regent, would have continued the godly demeanor of his father, but such was not to be.

## THE BEGINNING OF THE END

### 2 Kings 21:1-26

THE REIGN OF MANASSEH (21:1-18)

The Southern Kingdom was to be ruled by six kings before the

9. Merrill F. Unger, *Unger's Bible Dictionary*, p. 481.
10. Ibid., 481-82.

end would come. Of these six, all except one were judged to be "evil in the sight of the Lord." But of the five so evaluated, Manasseh and his son Amon were the worst.

## Manasseh's accession (21:1-9)

Manasseh's reign began when, as a youngster of twelve, he was placed on the throne as a co-ruler with his father Hezekiah. That Manasseh failed to follow the godly example of his father is perplexing. He had begun his co-regency in 698 B.C. and was sole ruler from the time of Hezekiah's death in 686 B.C. until 643 B.C. when his son served as co-regent for a short period.

All that Hezekiah had reformed, Manasseh reinstituted. From the description of his religious degradation, one wonders if any vile practice of heathendom was excluded: the worship of the Phoneician deities, Baal worship, the Chaldean-like astrological worship, and the Ammonite worship of Molech in which Ahaz before him had engaged. In addition the Temple was desecrated by the erection of an Asherah image.

All this would be the formal evidence in Jehovah's indictment against the people of Judah, for, in spite of the promise made to David and Solomon (vv. 7-8), there was the attendant warning against departure from the Law.

## Manasseh rebuked (21:10-15)

So through His prophets, God delivered His sentence:

> Behold, I am bringing such calamity on Jerusalem and Judah, that whoever hears of it, both his ears shall tingle. And I will stretch over Jerusalem the line of Samaria and the plummet of the house of Ahab, and I will wipe Jerusalem as one wipes a dish, wiping it and turning it upside down. And I will abandon the remnant of My inheritance and deliver them into the hand of their enemies, and they shall become as plunder and spoil to all their enemies (21:12-14).

Manasseh failed to learn from the histories of his predecessors, both in Judah and in the fallen Northern Kingdom. God's records finally were such that nothing was left but punishment.

### Manasseh's repentance (2 Chron 33:10-17)

The record in Chronicles adds a refreshing note to the account of this man. He was taken captive by the Assyrians and taken away to Babylon. As many after him, he was cured of idolatry in the capital of idolatry. When his captivity occurred is not known but while in Babylon, Manasseh recognized the Lord. He prayed for deliverance; God answered and allowed Manasseh to return to Judah. The restored king then cleansed the house of the Lord and removed certain pagan altars, though the "high places" were allowed to remain as places to worship Jehovah.

### Manasseh's death (21:16-18)

All that the recorder of Kings remembered, was the evil Manasseh had brought upon the inhabitants of Judah. When he died he was succeeded by a son who had learned only his father's evil ways.

### THE REIGN OF AMON (21:19-26)

The short reign of Amon was two years long. The Jehovist party seems to have gained enough strength to bring about the assassination of the king, though this was not a popular move (v. 24). Even the record in Chronicles is abbreviated. The lesson learned is that "he forsook the LORD . . . and did not walk in the way of the LORD" (v. 22).

## THE EYE OF THE STORM

### 2 Kings 22:1—23:30

An outstanding king halted the execution of God's judgment for a time. Josiah was a lad of only eight when his father Amon died at age twenty-four. Josiah shares with Hezekiah and Asa the distinction of being one of Judah's greatest kings. Scripture says their lives were patterned after the life of David.

JOSIAH'S ACCESSION (22:1-2)

The writer first presents the simple formula which gives the data relevant to Josiah's reign. Josiah began his reign late in 641 B.C., and his rule ended just four years before Nebuchadnezzar came to Judah and carried off the first captives.

JOSIAH'S REFORMS (22:3—23:25)

The record is paralleled by the account in 2 Chronicles 34—35. The first seventeen years of Josiah's reign were left without comment in the Kings record. The recorder of Chronicles notes, that in the eighth year of his reign, Josiah began to "seek the God of his father David." In the twelfth year of his rule, Josiah began to purge Jerusalem of the idolatrous elements promoted by Amon. Evidently, this purge continued until those influences were eradicated.

In his eighteenth year, the work of restoring the Temple began. While refurbishing the house of the Lord, Hilkiah the high priest discovered the book of the Law in the Temple. Exactly what he found has from time to time been a source of great discussion. Very possibly it was a copy of the Pentateuch, called by the Hebrew name *Torah* in the Hebrew text. The book was given to the royal scribe, Shaphan, who, in turn, took it to the king and began to read it.

The hearing of the words of Torah brought a swift response from Josiah. We are given insight at this point as to the ignorance of the people of God. Though led by a king whose heart was right toward Jehovah, nevertheless, there was no knowledge of what God had said to His people. The king commanded that a prophetic voice be heard regarding the words of judgment that the scribe had read.

A committee went to a prophetess named Huldah. She informed them that the words of judgment would come to pass, but that Josiah would be spared from those calamitous events because his heart was right.

After hearing this message, Josiah's next action was to assemble the people and read for them all the words of the recovered book. The portions read were probably those from Deuteronomy, which note the blessings and cursings echoed from Mount Ebal and Mount Gerizim (Deut 27—28).

Josiah's reforms resembled those carried out by his great-grandfather, Hezekiah. He eliminated not only the objects of idolatrous worship but also eradicated the priests who had led the people into these corrupt practices. In addition to the reforms that he led in Judah, Josiah also traveled to Bethel and there destroyed the high place that Jeroboam I had constructed. First Kings 13:2 contains the prophetic prediction that this altar would be destroyed and its attendants sacrificed by a Judean king, Josiah. But the priests who attended this altar were now dead. How then could the word of God be fulfilled literally? Josiah took their bones from the graves and burned them upon the altar.

As Hezekiah before him had done, he reinstituted the Passover feast. This feast was so elaborate that it stood alone in the remembrance of the recorder. The details concerning the great feast are given in 2 Chronicles 35:1-19. The record states, "There had not been celebrated a Passover like it in Israel since the days of Samuel the prophet; nor had any of the kings of Israel celebrated such a Passover as Josiah did with the priests, the Levites, all Judah and Israel who were present, and the inhabitants of Jerusalem" (2 Chron 35:18). The offerings of lambs and goats alone numbered 30,000, plus 3,000 bulls (2 Chron 35:7).

JUDAH'S JUDGMENT REITERATED (23:26-27)

But all the revival in Josiah's reign would not result in the dismissal of Jehovah's charges against Judah. The writer recalled the words of judgment which remind the reader again of the consequences of persistent disobedience.

JOSIAH'S DEATH IN BATTLE (23:28-30)

Pharaoh Necho ruled Egypt from 609-593 B.C. In his first year, he moved northward to aid the Assyrians after their capital Nineveh had fallen to the Babylonians in 612 B.C. But the Assyrians were not through. A token state remained in the ancient biblical city of Haran until even this was destroyed by the Babylonians in 610 B.C. Josiah, who may have been pursuing a pro-Babylonian policy, nevertheless recognized the Egyptian movement as a threat to his own kingdom. Josiah consequently engaged Necho in battle at Megiddo. The result was disastrous. Josiah was killed, and his body was transported back to Jerusalem, where he was buried. With his death, all hope of spiritual revival was gone. The events that followed his reign would rapidly bring down the proud Judean capital.

### THE RENEWED FURY AND DESTRUCTION

#### 2 Kings 23:31—25:30

The chronology of the latter part of this period revolves around captivities. Josiah's successor, Jehoahaz, was taken prisoner in the year of his father's death (609 B.C.). Consequently, another son of Josiah, Jehoiakim, succeeded him and ruled about twelve years. During his reign, captives were carried off to Babylon in 605 B.C. and again in 597 B.C. and 586 B.C. The late date marks the end of the Southern Kingdom, and the end of any independent Jewish state until May 14, 1948.

THE REIGN OF JEHOAHAZ (23:31-33)

The three-month reign of Josiah's eldest son, Jehoahaz, was marked as "evil." It seems incredible that he could have made such a mark in three short months. But it should be remembered that the evaluation of a particular king was based upon his attitude toward the house of the Lord. This is implied in the record of Kings and is the central theme in Chronicles.

Pharaoh Necho, returning from the north, made Judah a vassal kingdom under Egypt. This resulted in the imprisonment of Jehoahaz and the establishment of a brother, Eliakim, in his place. Eliakim means "whom God has set." His name was changed to Jehoiakim, which means "whom Jehovah has set." To Necho, the name of God, *El,* was more significant than the short form of *Yah* since *Yahweh* was, he felt, merely a local deity, whereas *El* was recognized as supreme. Necho probably changed Eliakim's name to show authority over him.

The end of Jehoahaz was lamented by the contemporary prophet Jeremiah. He referred to him as Shallum, and mourned using these words:

> Do not weep for the dead or mourn for him,
> But weep continually for the one who goes away;
> For he will never return
> Or see his native land (Jer 22:10).

## THE REIGN OF JEHOIAKIM (23:34—24:7)

A puppet of Egypt, Jehoiakim found his alliances shifting suddenly. Coming to power in 609 B.C., he became the vassal of Babylon in only four years. His eleven-year reign was one of subservience to the rival powers who marched unopposed through his land. Egypt was defeated in the battle of Carchemish in 605 B.C. Following the battle, the crown prince of Babylon, Nebuchadnezzar, marched his forces south and placed Judah under Babylonian control. Nebuchadnezzar became the Babylonian monarch at the death of his father in 604 B.C. Judah was saved by the events in Babylonia, but rebelled three years later by failing to send tribute and aligned herself with Egypt. In spite of warnings of Jeremiah, Judah continued pursuit of pagan alliances which led ultimately to disaster.

Jehoiakim's kingdom was besieged by marauding bands from all over the east, and he was powerless to stop them. Jehoiakim was taken as a prisoner to Babylon.

### THE REIGN OF JEHOIACHIN (24:8-16)

Jehoiakim's son Jehoiachin ruled Judah three months. Jehoiakin is also known as Coniah in Scripture. Although he had a brief reign, Jehoiachin achieved notoriety by his actions against the Lord. Jeremiah pronounced that he was the last king in a direct line from Solomon who would ever rule over Judah.

> "Thus says the Lord,
> 'Write this man down childless,
> A man who will not prosper in his days;
> For no man of his descendants will prosper
> Sitting on the throne of David
> Or ruling again in Judah' " (Jer 22:30).

Jehoiachin and many of the nobility were taken as prisoners to Babylon. Carried away with them were the palace and Temple treasures. All that was left to Judah was a remnant that was not considered useful to the Babylonian monarch.

### THE REIGN OF ZEDEKIAH (24:17—25:21)

The eleven-year reign of Jehoiachin's uncle Zedekiah was also marked by rebellion against Babylon. It appears that Josiah's successors were slow learners. As a result, in 586 B.C., Nebuchadnezzar besieged Jerusalem. After eighteen months of siege, the city was broken into and completely destroyed. Zedekiah's sons were slaughtered before him and, to fix this as a lasting reminder of the penalty for rebellion, the Babylonian conquerors put out his eyes and took him prisoner to Babylon. With the exception of the poorest farmers, the people were led away into exile. The Temple treasures were carried off, the last eruptions of resistance were snuffed out, and "so Judah was led away into exile from its land" (25:21).

## THE DESOLATION

### 2 Kings 25:22-30

Little was left. Only the poorest of farmers remained. Nebuchadnezzar appointed Gedaliah as their governor. But some still rebelled. Ishmael, a member of the royal family, conspired to kill the Babylonian governor, and many of the inhabitants fled to Egypt for safety. The account of Kings ends with the land decimated. Although King Jehoiachin was released, he remained a house prisoner of the Babylonian ruler for the rest of his life.

### EPILOGUE

What lesson can be learned from these books? What application can be made for today? Are conditions really so different? Is there not, in this time, a substitution of other items in the place that God should occupy? Is there not a dearth of interest in and knowledge of the Word of God?

This present decade has been one of intense religious activity, and the reader should recognize anew that the Israelites also experienced periods of "religious activity." But there were few genuine revivals, that is, movements back to an obedience to Torah (the Law). The study of 1 and 2 Kings, then, brings a stark reminder that sinfulness can coexist with mere religious interest. Genuine revival is accompanied by an inner change— one such as characterized Isaiah during the dark days of Ahaz's rule (Isa 6:1-7).

Happily, the books of the Kings do not complete the account of God's working with His people. The dark tones of captivity were brightened with the announcement half a millennium later that Messiah had come. Man could have a new birth. The servitude to sin could end because of a faithful God who graciously acted in behalf of all men through the gift of His Son—the Scion of David—Jesus of Nazareth.

# OLD TESTAMENT KINGS AND PROPHETS

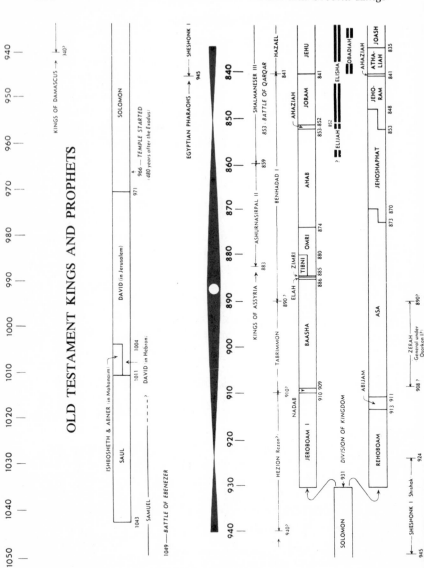

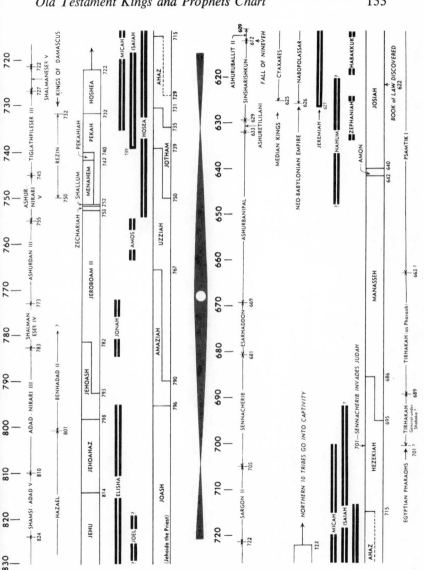

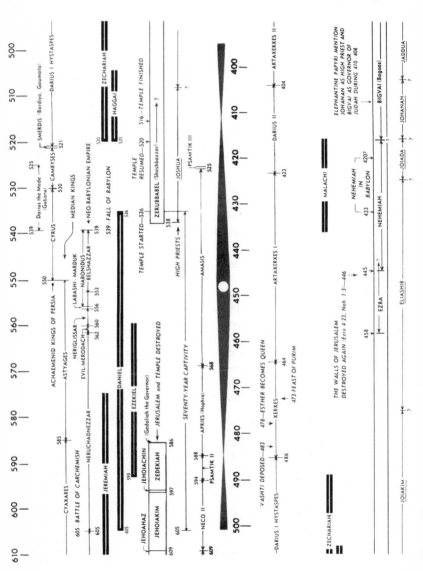

# Bibliography

Albright, William F. *The Biblical Period from Abraham to Ezra.* New York: Harper & Row, 1963.

Alexander, David, and Alexander, Pat, eds. *Eerdmans' Handbook to the Bible.* Grand Rapids: Eerdmans, 1973.

Archer, Gleason L. *A Survey of Old Testament Introduction.* Chicago: Moody, 1964.

Augustine. *The Confessions of St. Augustine.* Translated by E. B. Pusey. The Harvard Classics, vol. 7. New York: Collier & Son, 1909.

Deissman, Adolf. *Light from the Ancient East.* Grand Rapids: Baker, 1965.

Finegan, Jack. *Light from the Ancient Past.* Princeton, N.J.: U. Press, 1959.

Glueck, Nelson. *Rivers in the Desert.* New York: Grove, 1959.

Gray, John. *I and II Kings.* Philadelphia: Westminster, 1970.

Harrison, Roland K. *Introduction to the Old Testament.* Grand Rapids: Eerdmans, 1971.

Jamieson, Robert; Fausset, Andrew R.; and Brown, David, eds. *A Commentary, Critical, Experimental and Practical on the Old and New Testaments.* 6 vols. Grand Rapids: Eerdmans, 1961. Vol. 2. *Joshua-Esther,* by Robert Jamieson; Vol. 3, *Job-Isaiah,* by A. R. Fausset.

Keil, C. F. and Franz Delitzsch, eds. *Biblical Commentary on the Old Testament.* 25 vols. Grand Rapids: Eerdmans, n.d. Vol. 6, *The Books of the Kings,* by C. F. Keil.

Krummacher, Friedrich W. *Elisha.* Grand Rapids: Zondervan, n.d.

Lewis, Jack P. *Historical Backgrounds of Bible History.* Grand Rapids: Baker, 1971.

Maclear, G. F. *A Class Book of Old Testament History.* Grand Rapids: Eerdmans, 1959.

Merrill, Eugene H. *An Historical Survey of the Old Testament.* Nutley, N.J.: Craig, 1971.

Montgomery, James A. *A Critical and Exegetical Commentary on the Books of Kings.* Edited by H.`S. Gehman. The International Critical Commentary. Edinburgh: T. & T. Clark, 1967.

Morgan G. Campbell. *The Unfolding Message of the Bible.* Westwood, N.J.: Revell, 1961.

Oehler, Gustav F. *Theology of the Old Testament.* Grand Rapids: Zondervan, n.d.

Orr, James, ed. *The International Standard Bible Encyclopedia.* 5 vols. Grand Rapids: Eerdmans, 1957.

Pfeiffer, Charles F. *Old Testament History.* Grand Rapids: Baker, 1973.

Price, Ira M.; Sellers, Ovid R.; and Carlson, E. Leslie. *The Monuments and the Old Testament.* Philadelphia: Judson, 1958.

Pritchard, James B. *Ancient Near Eastern Texts Relating to the Old Testament.* Princeton: U. Press, 1955.

Schultz, Samuel J. *The Old Testament Speaks.* New York: Harper & Row, 1960.

Scroggie, William G. *The Unfolding Drama of Redemption.* 3 vols. Grand Rapids: Zondervan, 1972.

Stiles, Mervin. *Synchronizing Hebrew Originals from Available Records.* 8 vols. Aptos, Calif.: photo reproduction, 1974-76.

Thiele, Edwin R. *The Mysterious Numbers of the Hebrew Kings.* Grand Rapids: Eerdmans, 1965.

Thompson, John A. *The Bible and Archaeology.* Grand Rapids: Eerdmans, 1962.

Turner, George A. *Historical Geography of the Holy Land.* Grand Rapids: Baker, 1973.

Unger, Merrill F. *Archaeology and the Old Testament.* Grand Rapids: Zondervan, 1974.

Unger, Merrill F. *Unger's Bible Dictionary.* Chicago: Moody, 1961.

Wood, Leon. *A Survey of Israel's History.* Grand Rapids: Zondervan, 1973.